DB2 pureScale
Risk Free Agile Scaling

About the Authors

Paul C. Zikopoulos, B.A., M.B.A., is the Director of Technical Professionals for IBM Software Group's Information Management division. In this role, he has executive responsibilities for the vitality of its client-facing technical professional community and ensuring they're among the most technically skilled personnel in the marketplace. In his previous role, Paul led the DB2 Evangelist and DB2 Competitive programs for IBM. Paul is an award-winning writer and speaker with more than 18 years of experience in Information Management. Paul has written more than 300 magazine articles and 14 books on DB2, including *Break Free with DB2 9.7: A Tour of Cost Saving Features; Information on Demand: Introduction to DB2 9.5 New Features; DB2 Fundamentals Certification for Dummies; DB2 for Dummies;* and more. Paul is a DB2 Certified Advanced Technical Expert (DRDA and Clusters) and a DB2 Certified Solutions Expert (BI and DBA). In his spare time, he enjoys all sorts of sporting activities, including running with his dog Chachi, avoiding punches in his MMA training, and trying to figure out the world according to Chloë—his daughter. You can reach him at: paulz_ibm@msn.com.

Matt Huras, B.ASc., M.Eng., is an IBM Distinguished Engineer, and a senior architect for the DB2 on the Linux, UNIX, and Windows platform. He focuses on the database kernel, which includes the data management, index management, locking, concurrency, and other protocols. Matt has been with IBM for 26 years and has a Bachelor of Applied Science from the University of Waterloo and a Master of Engineering from the University of Toronto. Matt's most recent project role was the lead architect of DB2 pureScale—a new feature focusing on delivering new levels of scalability and availability.

Paul Awad, B.Sc., is an IBM Product Manager whose main focus is DB2 pureScale. Paul has been with IBM for 9 years and before that earned a Bachelor of Science from Dalhousie University (Nova Scotia, Canada). Paul has held several leadership positions while at IBM, including roles in support, the Project Office, and the Collaboration Center. Paul is currently the DB2 pureScale Product Manager, and in this role he has influence over the DB2 pureScale product, customer, and market feedback channels for the offering as well as enabling the product to market.

Aamer Sachedina, B.Eng., P.Eng., is a Senior Technical Staff Member and IBM Master Inventor at the IBM Toronto Lab. Over the years, he contributed to the design of the DB2 kernel, was the architect of DB2's Automatic Storage, and most recently headed the active-active availability effort as the HA architect on the DB2 pureScale project. In addition, some of Aamer's other passionate interests include: the dog sport of Schutzhund (which he participates in with his Belgian Tervuren "Farrah" and an up-and-coming Belgian Malinos puppy, Griffin) and breeding and maintaining a herd of Scottish Galloway cattle at his hobby farm with his lovely wife Jen and their two boys, Hayden and Julian.

DB2 pureScale

Risk Free Agile Scaling

Paul Zikopoulos
Matthew Huras
Paul Awad
Aamer Sachedina

New York   Chicago   San Francisco
Lisbon   London   Madrid   Mexico City
Milan   New Delhi   San Juan
Seoul   Singapore   Sydney   Toronto

McGraw-Hill books are available at special quantity discounts to use as premiums and sales promotions, or for use in corporate training programs. To contact a representative, please e-mail us at bulksales@mcgraw-hill.com.

DB2 pureScale: Risk Free Agile Scaling

1 2 3 4 5 6 7 8 9 0   DOC DOC   1 0 9 8 7 6 5 4 3 2 1 0

ISBN   978-0-07-175240-4
MHID   0-07-175240-4

The pages within this book were printed on paper containing 100% post-consumer fiber.

Sponsoring Editor
Roger Stewart

Editorial Supervisor
Patty Mon

Project Manager
Vasundhara Sawhney,
Glyph International

Acquisitions Coordinator
Joya Anthony

Copy Editor
Margaret Berson

Proofreader
Paul Tyler

Production Supervisor
Jean Bodeaux

Composition
Glyph International

Illustration
Glyph International

Art Director, Cover
Jeff Weeks

After 14 books, I won't promise not to write any more since I always seem to break that promise and tell you about it here. Professionally, I want to dedicate this book to the executives who helped me before and after my executive appointment: Picciano, Passarelli, Wildberger, Rivot, Vella, King, Keane, Salkeld, and Krishna have all given me tremendous guidance (and hopefully more in the future since I'm thanking them so publicly!). Why the last name references? I've played sports at an elevated level my whole life. Well, it seems like someone else's life now that I'm older; nevertheless, that's how folks generally refer to people on a team—and it's truly a team I'm proud to play on. These folks have always operated in a manner whereby it's not about their success, rather the success of the people around us and in turn, our business; again, tremendous guidance.

Personally, to my mother-in-law; yes, you read that right. Not a lot of sons-in-law make that dedication, I bet. My mother-in-law has vitality for life and she fought really hard to keep it in a recent and very sobering scare. An inspiration to many—for Nancy Doyle.

Finally, for my **petaloutha** *(Greek for butterfly), who is still the darling little angel that spat up all over me within minutes of our first meeting and is my strength: Chloë Alyse Zikopoulos; my life couldn't be right without her. I hope when she grows up and I'm no longer cool, she'll read these dedications and think I am... or was.*

I feel it also prudent to thank Debbie McAmmond at Air Canada who somehow seems to keep me flying like an nut which is when I find the time to write my books.

—Paul Zikopoulos

Dedicated to my wife Theresa, son Adam, and daughter Katie—I could not imagine what it would be like without your constant support during my many long hours on this project. And, I'd like to extend a heartfelt thanks as well as congratulations to all the members of the DB2 pureScale team across all organizations, divisions, and geographies. Your efforts have been heroic, and the end result, astounding.

—Matt Huras

I dedicate this book to my two beautiful boys; without their support, love, and hugs, I wouldn't have been able to achieve many of the things I do, including this book. I am lucky and grateful to have them in my life.

—Paul Awad

This book is dedicated to my beloved wife Jen and our two boys—Hayden and Julian—without whose support I couldn't finish the things I do (at work, at the farm, and with the dogs). Thank you for letting me pursue my passions and for putting up with all the idiosyncrasies that come with them. I also want to extend a heartfelt thanks to the DB2 pureScale development team at large and in particular the Recovery Orchestration and Cluster Management development team, which I led. We could never have accomplished what we did if it were not for your unrelenting efforts.

—Aamer Sachedina

CONTENTS AT A GLANCE

CONTENTS

ACKNOWLEDGMENTS

Collectively, we want to thank the following people without whom this book would not have been possible: Andrew Buckler, Serge Boivin, Yvonne Chan, Miso Cilimdzic, Chris Eaton, Christian Garcia, Terrie Jacopi, Aslam Nomani, Sal Vella, Martin Wildberger, Irshad Raihan, Steve Rees, Jessica Rockwood, Glen Sheffield, Michael Springgay, Frankie Sun, and Aimin Wu. Finally, to our publishing team: lead by Joya Anthony, Lisa McClain, Roger Stewart, and our terrific project manager Vasundhara Sawhney—the extra week came in handy!

ABOUT THIS BOOK

We're pretty sure you've figured out that this book is about one of the most exciting technologies to come out of the IBM research and development labs: DB2 pureScale. This book was written to give readers a business and technical introduction to the value of DB2 pureScale, its differentiating characteristics, and its "under-the-cover" operations. In consideration of the limited amount of space we had, we had to make some tough trade-offs and cutoff points, and while no author was hurt in this process, it wasn't easy. We believe we've created a book that should give you a strong overview of the DB2 pureScale technology and its key tenets, which deliver unprecedented levels of agility, scalability, and availability to your distributed environment.

In Chapter 1, "An Introduction to DB2 pureScale: The Value Proposition," we talk about the business-related aspect that a DB2 pureScale solution can deliver to your IT infrastructure. From discussions about cloud-like per-day pricing, to transparent scaling, and continuous availability, after reading this chapter you'll be left thinking, "Okay, sounds good, now prove it." Chapter 2, "DB2 pureScale Performance Results: What Your Business Can Finally Realize," is where we indeed prove it by presenting you with examples that demonstrate the transparent scalability architecture that DB2 pureScale provides.

After reading Chapter 2, you're probably going to be wondering what a DB2 pureScale solution looks like, and indeed, we cover that in Chapter 3, "DB2 pureScale Key Concepts: A Primer for the Rest of the Book." Chapter 3 will introduce you to terms such as member, interrupt-free RMDA (it's a differentiator, so remember it), cluster caching facility, InfiniBand, and more. Not familiar with those terms? Read the chapter!

The rest of the book answers the questions that surround "How does it work?" Chapter 4, "Transparent Application Scaling with DB2 pureScale," delves into the DB2 pureScale "secret sauce," its force-at-commit protocol, and other things that allow it to achieve the results outlined in Chapter 2 *without* changing the application! Chapter 5, "DB2 pureScale Configuration: The Operational 101," is really tailored to database administrators (DBAs) and talks about some of the configuration aspects of a DB2 pureScale operational environment. We were reluctant to include this chapter since we wanted to stick to how the DB2 pureScale technology works as opposed to its operational aspects, but we figured we could help some DBAs to pick up the technology faster if we did. Chapter 6, "DB2 pureScale for Availability," will introduce you to all the amazing high-availability features that are part of DB2 pureScale; you'll learn about things we call split brain, fencing, DB2 Cluster Services, and how DB2 pureScale doesn't have to freeze I/O to the database (like competing products) to recover from typical software and hardware failures. Finally, in Chapter 7, "DB2 pureScale Workload Balancing and Automatic Client Reroute," we talk about the built-in workload balancer algorithm that's enabled by default for all DB2 pureScale installations; in addition, how DB2 pureScale can move a single transaction on a host computer in a DB2 pureScale cluster that failed to another host computer in the cluster and restart it without returning an error to the application—now that's cool!

Again, we couldn't cover everything in this book because we didn't want to create numbered volumes for it. But we feel we've given you enough to truly appreciate this wonderful technology. Enjoy!

DB2 pureScale

Risk Free Agile Scaling

Part I

From the Business Perspective

1

An Introduction to DB2 pureScale: The Value Proposition

In today's ever-changing business landscape, information technology (IT) organizations are under enormous pressures to handle increasingly complex workloads in a continuously available manner. They're also responsible to ensure that an agreed-upon level of performance—referred to as the *service level agreement* (SLA)—is strictly maintained. Quite simply, if a solution isn't performing at the transaction rate defined in the SLA, that solution is considered not available; for good reason, your clients will go elsewhere.

As the voracious appetite for smart Internet device connectivity expands, enterprises are driving more and more back-office applications to the "glass" via online web portals, self-service mobile applications, and more. For example, think about your day-to-day banking activities over the last two decades. We've seen its forms move from face-to-face interactions, to ATMs, and to desktops and laptops, with the latest conduit being mobile applications on your favorite smart mobile devices. In addition, the banking functions at your fingertips' disposal continually expand (though perhaps it isn't a good thing to be able to apply for more credit while you're in the middle of a tarmac delay). There are certain IT consequences that stem from these trends in that more and more applications are SLA-governed, and as a consequence there are a greater number of consumer touch points with bigger availability and performance expectations, more frequent troughs and valleys in required compute power,

3

and much more. What's more, as more and more applications get on the executive team's "radar," the verbiage used to describe their associated maintenance windows has morphed from overnight, to shrinking, to almost nonexistent—all of which make the current IT environment that much more complex and harder to manage.

Let's add to the mix the world's most despised catch phrase: "Do more with less." We've never liked this phrase because it always meant less vacation for us; with that said, there's no question that in today's IT environment, we're asked to get more done, while at the same time many seem to be losing the resources and agility to do just that.

We've all been through project planning cycles, but the reality is that plans are in constant flux and are heavily affected by market volatility, which makes it difficult to accurately forecast workload volumes years in advance; ironically, our capital allocation budgets seem to demand such accurate (and perhaps psychic) forecasts. The result of this conundrum is a competitive advantage for those companies that can smartly sense and easily respond to changing workload volumes with dynamic capacity allocations delivered in a utility-like fashion. Think about it: When you go to bed at night, do you leave all the lights on? Of course not, so why have you statically overallocated loads of capacity to your database server in order to handle just a couple of high traffic days when workload demands are so briefly disproportionate compared to the rest of the year? At the same time, when you need light, you don't go into your basement and install a fuse before turning on your room light for the few minutes you need it, turn the light off when finished, then go back downstairs and remove the fuse, do you? Hopefully not; so why would you accept risky and lengthy development cycles to change your application in order to respond to capacity requirements? Finally, you depend on the fact that when you go into your room and flip a light switch, that light is going to brighten the room; so your resources need to be dependable and robust as well.

Businesses can greatly benefit from an agile IT infrastructure that can help them do more with less. For example, as an application's benefits become more critical to the business, its requirements increase and become more stringent, thereby requiring more performance and availability. As a consequence, the IT environment hosting such an application has to be agile and flexible enough to adapt. If you're in the retail game in the United States, the Black Friday (the first Friday that follows the American Thanksgiving holiday) drain on the IT infrastructure outstrips the rest of the year by a long shot. If you're a global retail vendor and you service Canada as well, the retail "home run" day is actually Boxing Day (December 26th). In a "do more with less" economy, surely you don't want to overallocate all of your precious resources for a couple of days' requirements and then be overallocated for the rest of the year, wasting precious resources (leave the lights on when you're not in the room per our analogy). Added capacity should be flexible enough that you only pay for it on the days you use it (which you can do with DB2 pureScale) and agile enough that adding and removing capacity to your environment is transparent and doesn't require risky changes to the application (you don't tinker with the fuse box to enable more lights—you just plug a lamp into the wall). In this retail example, perhaps in the final quarter, between Canadian and U.S.-based retail sales, there are two 6-day resource spikes, with perhaps 30 days between them. Some retail businesses allocate the resources required to handle the known 6-day spikes for an entire year. Others painstakingly tinker with the environment in the quarters before and after to try to deliver the extra capacity for the quarter (and take a lot of risk doing so). A business grounded in smart computing uses a technology that allows you to seamlessly move in more compute power for the initial 6-day spike (Black Friday in the United States), remove it, then add it again one month later for the Canadian spike (Boxing Day) and just pay for the extra resources required for those 12 days (like you can with DB2 pureScale). The bottom line is that today's businesses need sensory-driven infrastructure changes that can be implemented in a risk-free, easy, and fast manner.

Of course, today's business landscape is also an ever-changing one, and as local databases become global, there's even more pressure on those previously mentioned SLAs, with peak times seeming to arrive in unexpected waves from around the globe; we refer to this as the *velocity* of data. We could go on; for example, the sheer *volume* of data being stored is growing so rapidly that it's no longer a keynote opener to comment on data growth rates in correlation to the amount of information in the U.S. Library of Congress, or how many trips to the moon and back would be generated each day if this information were not digitized. We could note that you could step away from all these IT challenges and remind yourself that IT isn't there because it's fun to buy software and hardware; it's there to help the business execute its mission statement. We won't talk about all these things (and more). Why? You likely know much of this and we'll start to sound like Billy Joel's "We Didn't Start the Fire" song. It's sufficient to say that while the current IT climate is one that can be described as exciting, capable, and opportunistic, historically it's also one of the most challenging eras for IT, and something different is needed for distributed systems such as Linux or UNIX. Enter DB2 pureScale.

DB2 pureScale Core Values

DB2 pureScale is an optional DB2 feature that reduces the risks and costs associated with business growth and IT departments seeking "true" agility, by providing application transparency, unlimited capacity, and continuous availability across a cluster of database servers that all share a common set of disks (it's implemented as shared-disk architecture).

NOTE   *DB2 pureScale became generally available as DB2 9.8 in 2009. The only reason you would migrate from a DB2 9.7 environment to DB2 9.8 is if you want to leverage the DB2 pureScale technology; otherwise, you would stay on the DB2 9.7 maintenance stream. These releases likely will merge under a common version in the future.*

Application Transparency

DB2 pureScale allows businesses to avoid the risks and costs associated with application changes by allowing them to transparently change the capacity characteristics of their database clusters. We're going to be blunt here: There are competing solutions whose marketing slogans claim that their cluster software scales transparently, but there's an abundance of proof points and best practices that suggest you have to change your applications to be "cluster-aware" if you want their solution to scale efficiently. We're not suggesting that these solutions can't be made to scale. Anything can demonstrate performance *if* you have an unlimited budget and don't care about efficiency. But that's more like a Facebook community farming or restaurant game than it is reality. Since we're not playing Clusterville here, we'll note that losing limited resources to lots of manual work, and adding in all sorts of risk associated with application changes, doesn't just wither or spoil the environment; it costs serious real dollars. These required application changes introduce inefficiencies and risks into the environment that businesses shouldn't have to tolerate to simply add workload capacity to the underlying IT solution. Think about if you wanted to remove capacity from the cluster (so that you can be agile and not tie up your precious resources for an entire year when the higher capacity is only needed for a couple of days), you'd have to navigate the risky straits and high-cost waters all over again! When a lot of explicit manual work and the cost and risk associated with application changes can't be avoided, you need something different. DB2 pureScale is different.

If you were to interview a typical database administrator (DBA) and ask them how long it would take them to implement a production schema change—such as changing a column's data type—the answer typically varies between two and four weeks because of testing and deployment. If you can't comfortably change a production environment's column's data type in a timely manner, how long do you think it would take to change an application, perform required regression tests, and deploy those changes? DB2 pureScale allows you to add or remove capacity from a database cluster in a fully application-transparent manner; quite simply, you don't have to risk costly and manual changes to your applications or make them "cluster-aware" to get a decent scalability return on your investment: Just enter a simple command. That's a differentiator, and we invite you to move past the marketing veneer and spin that you're being bombarded with from certain competitors and try it out for yourself!

Unlimited Capacity That's Dynamic and Optionally Priced Per Day

Today's IT shops require smarter solutions that can quickly respond to the needs of their business; their infrastructure needs to be dynamic and allow them to scale quickly and effectively while doing so in a risk-free manner. When your executive branch plans the business, the sky is the limit (as it should be); we think the scalability of your database should match that view. DB2 pureScale allows you to start with a right-sized environment that meets current business needs and pretty much offers a practically no-limits scalability platform for your applications to grow. In fact, we've evalutated a 128-member cluster running DB2 pureScale, which is more processing power than any application that we know of could possibly require at this time. We'll show you this and some other proof points in Chapter 2.

DB2 pureScale's unlimited capacity is delivered in a flexible pay-as-you-go paradigm that allows clients to *add and remove* capacity that matches the fluctuation of their business: its cost structure is elastic. For example, consider a banking application whose capacity needs are managed by a cluster composed of three members; however, the final two weeks of the year are characterized by a massive spike of activity as investors rush to purchase tax-deferred investments.

It's during this two-week period that the business's capacity requirements grow from a three-member cluster to a five-member cluster.

DB2 pureScale enables businesses to add more compute capacity with a simple command and remove that temporary capacity from the cluster just as easily as the spike subsides. If the application permanently required the additional capacity, it could be transparently added as well, obviously. A key DB2 pureScale benefit includes the ability to license the software on a per-day basis, which provides significant savings for the business and delivers the scalability services offered by DB2 pureScale in a utility-like manner (you pay for your light's electricity when they are on, and you don't pay when they are off). In our banking example, the bank could simply light up two new servers in the cluster for the duration of the spike and then remove them at the end of that period, thereby saving them a lot of money (putting some "more" in the "with less" bucket). We should mention of course that you can also license DB2 pureScale in the same manner that you license all your other IBM software product—with a traditional perpetual license.

Continuous Availability

When discussing availability, one has to consider availability for planned outages to be as important as unplanned outages. DB2 pureScale delivers uninterrupted access to data with consistent performance.

DB2 pureScale enables businesses to recover automatically from unplanned failures. Consider a retail business with a three-member DB2 pureScale cluster: One of the three members fails due to some hardware or software problem. DB2 pureScale's built-in workload balancer algorithm automatically recognizes which members in the cluster are available and which aren't, and transparently distributes transactions around the failed member; what's more, some transactions can be transparently restarted on a surviving member in the cluster. At the same time, crash recovery for the failed member is automatically invoked and I/O to the database *is not* frozen; other solutions in the marketplace freeze access to the database's disk while lock information is remastered as well as some other recovery duties are prepped beyond REDO and UNDO processing. We're going to take you through all the details of this process in Chapter 6.

DB2 pureScale also provides availability scenarios for planned outages such as hardware- or operating system–based administration. As previously mentioned, the shrinking batch window environment that characterizes today's operational environments gives clients perhaps hours (if they're lucky) to perform such maintenance; however, these businesses need continuous access to their data, in a 24×7 fashion. DB2 pureScale allows a DBA to take a member out of the cluster without operationally impacting any running transactions. A DBA can drain-request a member, remove it from the cluster, and subsequently add it back as maintenance is performed in a rolling fashion across the cluster's members. A DB2 pureScale drain request causes the workload balancer algorithm to stop routing new incoming transactions to the target member and allows currently running transactions on that target member to end their life naturally (you can override this and force the transaction off the cluster if you want). In the meantime, the DB2 pureScale workload balancer algorithm will continue to send new transactions to the other members in the cluster. Once maintenance is done, the DBA reintroduces the member into the cluster, at which point the workload balancer algorithm recognizes it as transaction-eligible and begins to route work to it. This entire operation occurs without interruption to the application or data availability.

Consolidation

It's hard to attend any conference, read IT-focused collateral, or listen to a speech and not hear about *consolidation* in one form or another. From the cloud, to virtual pools, to dynamic partitions, a true path to cost savings is technology steeped in consolidation capability. In fact, we believe consolidation will be a dominant subject in the future and shows no indication of becoming obscure. After all, consolidation is also a key ingredient of business agility; as customers consolidate their environments, manage their key workloads, and automate their workflows, they are able to optimize the delivery of services and products with the agility and confidence to dynamically make risk-free changes to their environments in a short amount of time. The DB2 pureScale core values help clients pursue a true consolidation plan; they allow the CIO's office to stretch hardware and software utilization strategies and deliver a true just-in-time (JiT) capacity architecture that is ever available and scalable to match the needs of the business.

Where Does DB2 pureScale Come From?

Although DB2 pureScale is new technology for distributed DB2 servers, it's far from new. The DB2 pureScale technology is born from the proven DB2 for z/OS Parallel Sysplex architecture, which has been the recognized "gold" industry standard for maintaining critical applications' high availability and meeting scalability needs for more than 15 years. In fact, its reputation is so proven that even a competitor's CEO has noted that "it's a first-rate piece of technology."

Why such high regard for the parent DB2 pureScale technology? Simple: a piece of some pretty amazing technology within the Parallel Sysplex known as the *Coupling Facility (CF)*. The CF delivers high-availability and scalability services for DB2 Data Sharing environments on System z servers; it provides centralized locking and buffer caching services in order to reduce intracluster communication costs and provide instant awareness in the event of any component failures. DB2 for z/OS isn't the only mainframe technology that takes advantage of the CF facility. The entire environment, including IBM Customer Information Control System (CICS), IBM Information Management System (IMS), workload management, and much more, can leverage the CF, and that makes it even more unique to the System z platform.

The CF allows multiple processors to share, cache, update, and balance data access dynamically and leverages a hardware-based Server Time Protocol that synchronizes the clocks of all members in the system. The Parallel Sysplex's Global Resource Serialization technology allows multiple systems to access the same resources concurrently, serializing where necessary, to ensure exclusive access based on business requirements. Finally, the Parallel Sysplex is integrated with unique z/OS capabilities that provide robust clustering services including group management, intersystem messaging, and recovery management which ensure system-wide availability and security.

The bottom line is that the DB2 for z/OS Data Sharing and Parallel Sysplex have been running mission-critical enterprise applications since April 1994 with real-world leadership in availability, near-linear scalability, and performance, on the most secure platform on the planet. System z Parallel Sysplex technology was designed over 15 years ago specifically with online transaction processing (OLTP) in mind. It continues to evolve and set the bar for the most demanding, business-critical enterprise applications in the world.

Indeed, the DB2 pureScale technology inherits its key availability and scalability tenets from the DB2 for z/OS technology outlined in this section. DB2 pureScale is the first of its kind on distributed platforms such as UNIX and Linux. Make no mistake about it; if you're looking for the most scalable and available environment in the world, it's the mainframe. But DB2 pureScale allows you to deliver these values, for the first time ever, to the distributed platform. If you know a lot about DB2 for z/OS and its CF (referred to as the *cluster caching facility*—and uses the same acronym—in DB2 pureScale), you've got a really good idea how DB2 pureScale works (which we'll delve into in the remainder of this book).

Workload-Optimized Smart Solutions— Analytics or Transactions?

DB2 pureScale provides businesses with a practically unlimited capacity and ultra-available infrastructure for *transactional* workloads. That's something we want to make special note of in this section. While you can do some reporting-like workloads on it, DB2 pureScale has been *optimized* for transactional workloads. You may be familiar with the IBM Smart Analytics System (ISAS) for business analytics; these systems are *optimized* for analytic workloads and leverage a shared-nothing architecture. The emphasis around *optimized* is on purpose: Some vendors are trying to portray a single solution for every problem in the world when it comes to databases, but they neglect to mention that the characteristics of analytic and transactional solutions are very different.

The idea of designing and building things for a specific purpose is not new. For example, a Volkswagen Beetle, a city bus, and a Formula 1 race car can all drive people from point A to point B. But isn't one of these vehicles well suited for a daily commute, one exceptionally suited for racing, and one better for mass transit? IBM doesn't believe that a "one-size-fits-all" solution delivers the best value to our clients. For mass transit, would you use a two-seat sports car or a bus? Would you take your family to the movies in a city bus? Just as there are vehicles optimized for various transportation purposes, IBM believes that designing and building systems optimized from the ground up for specific workloads is the best approach. With this in mind, IBM has created workload-optimized systems that manage OLTP systems, warehouse systems, and mixed workloads in a way that saves clients money because they aren't forced to overbuy the environment which compensates for a lack of optimization. IBM understands the breadth and complexity of different workloads that enterprises face, and we know that a single-system approach can't satisfy diverse application requirements, especially solutions that compensate the lack of a shared-nothing architecture for certain workloads with a layer of disk software that you pay for to mimic a shared-nothing architecture. At the same time, customers want to run more and more transactional workload on their analytics systems and more analytics on their transactional systems.

For example, let's contrast online transaction processing (OLTP) and analytic systems. OLTP systems are used to run the business; these systems process the business transactions that are critical to any organization. Analytic systems use the data from OLTP systems to provide strategic and competitive differentiation in the marketplace, and to optimize business processes. The system characteristics, and therefore the architectural requirements, necessary to support OLTP systems and analytic systems are very different.

A smarter approach is to design and build systems for a specific purpose—this is the approach that IBM has taken with the IBM pureScale Application Server (IpAS) for OLTP workloads and the ISAS for analytic workloads. These smart systems focus on improving time-to-value with preconfigured components optimized for the appropriate workload. With a workload-optimized system, you end up with a system that delivers not just better performance—but the best price/performance ratio by avoiding components that are not relevant to the workload.

The ISAS is an integrated platform that provides broad analytics capabilities on a powerful data warehouse foundation with IBM servers and storage. Deeply integrated and optimized, ISAS provides a single control point for end-to-end analytics solutions: the industry's first pre-integrated analytics system designed to deploy quickly and flatten the time to value curve for this solution. This deeply optimized analytic system quickly delivers the insight you need to anticipate business conditions, capture new opportunities, avoid risks, and ultimately transform the way you operate to achieve greater profitability and competitive advantage. Unlike other data warehouse appliance vendor offerings, the ISAS includes the necessary software for end-user analytics. It is also broader in scope than what appliance vendors can offer, because underneath the analytic covers, the ISAS can support small data marts or the largest enterprise data warehouses, alongside built-in transformation capabilities, dimensional cubing services, and more.

The IpAS comes in an easily understandable and low-cost appliance solution (we'll delve into the details of the IpAS in the next section). The IpAS currently ships (as of the time this book was written) with two IBM Power 770 servers, each with 16 cores and 64GB of memory installed with all optimized connectivity (InfiniBand switches in this case with their associated adapters), and it is rack mounted.

The nice thing about IpAS and ISAS is that you get them in a "T-shirt size"–like methodology (extra small, small, medium, large, and extra large) that correlates to the demands of your application. If your application's demands require you to move between T-shirt sizes, this is a very simple thing to do in a safe and reliable manner (for IpAS it doesn't even require new hardware—how's that for risk free and fast!).

The problem with the "all things to all applications" approach taken by one of our competitors is that they are forcing the same hardware layout on customers for any workload; however, analytic and OLTP systems have *very different* I/O, storage, memory, and other characteristics. For example, characteristics for OLTP systems when compared to analytic systems include:

- Smaller database sizes that typically range from a few gigabytes to low terabytes as opposed to analytic databases that are measured in terabytes to petabytes

- I/O requirements that are primarily random I/O as opposed to sequential I/O often observed in analytic workloads

- Data is more likely to benefit from in-memory cache, whereas with data warehousing, the cache is often flushed as a result of millions of rows that compose intermediate results

- Transactions should minimize system resource usage (executing as few CPU instructions as possible) as opposed to leveraging a massively parallel infrastructure that tries to allocate as much resource as possible

- Transactional systems to scale compute power (CPU) independent of storage and I/O whereas analytic workloads have to be scaled in a balanced (CPU : I/O : Memory) manner

- Shared data architecture that can scale up and scale out is ideally suited for transaction-based OLTP workloads, whereas major players in analytics almost exclusively use shared-nothing

One vendor's offering doesn't map to these characteristics well at all. In fact, in a full-rack configuration, there is over 30 TB of storage that you are forced to buy, which is way too much for what you're likely trying to do if you are in the OLTP world. If you want to add more processing power (a primary driver of more resource for OLTP applications as opposed to more bias towards I/O throughput for analytic systems), you are forced to add more storage you don't need. What's more, you have to pay for database licenses on the storage as well as the servers with this vendor's offering; in other words, if you store more; you pay more, scale more, you pay more. In addition, this appliance's storage layer is effectively a shared-nothing storage server under a shared-disk database server, which adds more costs, complexity, and code path-length to transactions and therefore reduces scalability and throughput! Don't forget that you also have to pay for someone to manage all of this too.

Now consider if you wanted to grow your cluster. An IpAS solution comes with processors and memory already installed for a large configuration (if you bought a small one, these resources are simply not activated). This modality makes an upgrade very simple, fast, and reliable: You simply pay for the additional CPU, memory, and software that you need to "light" up versus the alternate one-size-fits-all approach that makes you buy, receive, install, cable, and configure additional hardware to grow the system.

IBM also offers Capacity on Demand (CoD) purchase rights for IpAS solutions, which makes the utility computing discussion earlier in this chapter a reality. You can literally purchase incremental IpAS capacity "by the day" to handle peak periods. That is, if you have a peak period of activity around a shopping holiday, you can turn on the additional capacity and buy DB2 pureScale "per day" licenses and hardware only for the days when you need the extra capacity. *Now that's agility!*

Optimized solutions focus on simplicity of the environment; after all, human error is the number one cause of downtime. The IpAS (*even* in a large configuration) is just two (albeit very powerful) POWER7 770 servers. That's a much easier solution to manage compared to the full rack of 8 database servers and 14 storage servers offered by the other vendor. For example, when you want to apply maintenance, what solution would be easier: 2 nodes or 22 nodes?

Now think about trying to pinpoint a problem in the system. If you wanted to scale such a solution, a two-node database cluster is much easier than an eight-node cluster. The point we are making here is that optimized solutions can't come up with a one-size-conquers-all paradigm. They are engineered from the core to the glass and their benefits far outweigh the alternate approach, which is more about throwing any amounts of resources at a solution and upping the cost.

The point of this section is to give you some things to think about that are often left out of impressive movie-linked marketing blitzes. Ever heard the saying, "That's only in the movies?"

The IBM pureScale Application System — Deeply Optimized for Transaction Workloads

The IBM pureScale Application System (IpAS) is a workload-optimized shared-disk active-everything database and application system targeted for transactional workloads. It incorporates the reliability and performance of IBM's DB2, WebSphere Application Server, Power 770 servers, and a cluster caching facility modeled after the DB2 for z/OS platform. Even before the IpAS was invented, DB2 and WebSphere Application Server were deeply optimized such that they exploit key POWER7 functionality that other software hasn't be designed to leverage to the best of our knowledge. Optimizations such as on-core decimal flotation arithmetic (especially useful for business transactions), memory protection keys (for robustness), workload management, reduction of memory footprint, and exploitation of active memory sharing, all lead to end-to-end application and resource management systems from IBM that is uniquely superior. DB2 even runs in a special WebSphere mode!

Customers ordering an IpAS solution can instantly inject the DB2 pureScale core value system into their operational environments because it's delivered in a pre-integrated, tested, and certified manner. This allows them to zero-slope their time-to-value curve with an order, plug-in, and experience delivery system.

The IpAS was also engineered from the ground up such that it delivers IT the maximum amount of agility when it comes to scaling; it allows you to scale out, up, or within in an application-transparent manner. As you can see in Figure 1.1, the IBM pureScale Application System allows businesses to start with a right-sized environment that grows with the needs of the business. It's a simple two-host computer environment that doesn't force-feed you more storage or compute capacity than you require. Customers can start right with an IpAS solution but maintain the capability to easily and quickly add capacity where it's needed, when it's needed.

The IBM pureScale Application System is based on the adaptable and flexible Power 770 server, which serves as a strong platform for reliability and consolidation of the environment. The IpAS is able to scale within by adding more cores, scale up by adding more drawers, or scale out by adding more Power 770 servers. For example, you can easily grow IpAS capacity by activating more cores (scale within) on each Power 770—up to 64 cores per box! You can

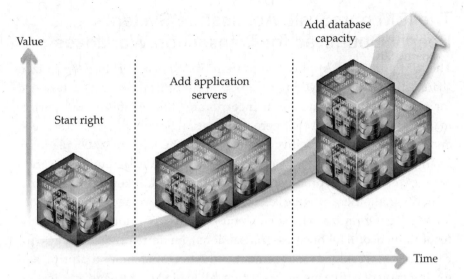

Figure 1.1 *Start right with the IBM pureScale Application System: now scale out, scale up, or scale within.*

also add to your system's capacity as the business outgrows its starting point by adding more Power 770 enclosures (scale up). Finally, additional Power 770 servers (scale out) can be added to system to handle peak capacity needs. These options are all shown in Figure 1.2.

An IpAS solution enables customers to consolidate many of their databases and applications into one environment, leading of course to reduced costs for power, cooling, and management. Since an IpAS comes set up, configured, and application ready, all an administrator needs to do is load their data and application, and they can go live. There's no need to rewrite or reconfigure the application, and the environment offers near-linear scalability, meaning the most effective use of the hardware and resource investment. Finally, you can order an IpAS with or without the WebSphere Application Server, depending on your needs.

A Brief Comment on Distributed DB2 Availability Options

The DB2 technology offers many different kinds of availability solutions that can be implemented for your business's availability needs. In the same manner in which IBM has invested in optimizing systems for specific business problems, we encourage clients to select the right DB2 availability technology

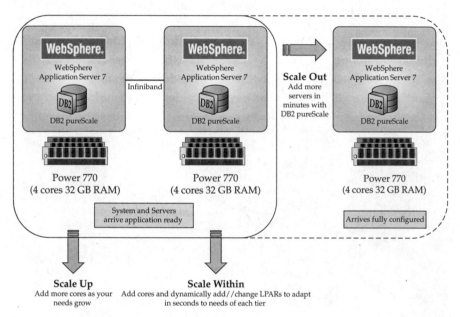

Figure 1.2 *An example of starting right—with multiple scaling options—using the IBM pureScale Application System*

for the business problem at hand as opposed to trying to use a one-size-fits-all approach for availability as well. In a typical enterprise, not every application needs the highest levels of availability. For some applications, the recovery point objective (RPOs) and recovery time objectives (RTOs) are very tight, while the SLAs applied to other applications' RTOs are measured in days. If an application is "allowed" to be down for a couple of days, to us, it doesn't make sense to enrich it with the most sophisticated availability technology on the market, unless of course your budgets allow you to do so.

As of DB2 9.8, there are four major availability options that are at your disposal: the integrated DB2 cluster manager; high-availability disaster recovery (HADR), which can be configured for read-on standby as of DB2 9.7; HADR with Q-Replication; and DB2 pureScale (which can also be implemented with Q-Replication). While it's outside the scope of this book to delve into the spectrum of availability options in a DB2 solution, we want you to be aware of them. For example, did you know that DB2 has a built-in cluster manager that you can configure in a hot/cold cluster and you don't have to pay for any standby database licenses or even the cluster manager software? This type of availability option is suitable for those applications that have very relaxed RTOs.

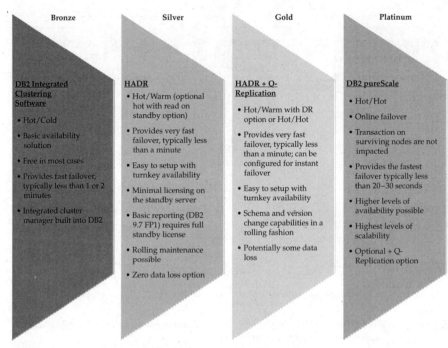

Figure 1.3 *A synopsis of availability options in DB2*

For a typical enterprise, we recommend that you take some time to enumerate your applications and place them in the appropriate tier that matches the commitment IT needs to make in order to support these applications from an availability perspective. Figure 1.3 gives a high-level summary of these options. Talk to your IBM representative for more information.

2

DB2 pureScale Performance Results: What Your Business Can Finally Realize

As we discussed in the previous chapter, DB2 pureScale serves as a transactional architecture that delivers virtually unlimited capacity, continuous availability, and transparent application scaling. In this chapter, before delving into the details of what a DB2 pureScale cluster looks like under the covers, we want to spend some time conveying to you some of the amazing performance and scalability results we've observed with this technology; namely, virtually unlimited capacity alongside transparent application scaling.

The Scalability Tests

The DB2 pureScale software was literally born out of clients' need to have an application-transparent transactionally optimized database that could scale near-linearly. Quite simply, such an option didn't truly exist on distributed platforms until DB2 pureScale. Indeed, DB2 pureScale enables administrators to dynamically scale their environments, up or down, and maintain these core values. Of course, we had a little help along the way: as you learned in Chapter 1, DB2 pureScale inherits its key availability and scalability tenets from the most available and scalable platform in the world: System z and its Sysplex architecture running DB2 for z/OS.

During the development of DB2 pureScale, our customers and the development labs took DB2 pureScale for a test drive; and not just any old test drive either.

We literally took DB2 pureScale where today's clusters just haven't been architecturally proven to go. We'll highlight two of these tests in this chapter. *None of the following tests had any cluster awareness or affinitization to members within the cluster (we're going to repeat ourselves on this point a lot because it is a big deal); we did not intervene* to distribute the workload across the cluster in a manner that balanced the load, the database wasn't tuned as more members were added, and so on. In other words, these scaling tests were transparent to the application, and all we did was add more and more members to the DB2 pureScale cluster.

The "More-Nodes-Than-You-Could-Ever-Imagine" Test

In this test (see Figure 2.1), we wanted to validate the DB2 pureScale architecture by assessing just how far it could scale. So, early on in the development cycle, we took some pre-release DB2 pureScale code and had the Toronto lab set up a DB2 pureScale cluster that started with a single member and dynamically grew the cluster to 128 members (since some of the biggest clusters in the world are on no more than 32 nodes, we figured this was quite the statement). To also demonstrate some of the consolidation capabilities of DB2 pureScale, we had some of the members virtualized and put multiple members on an SMP server.

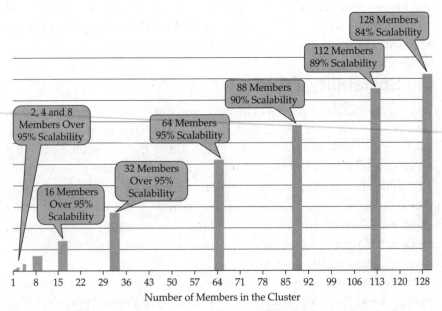

Figure 2.1 *A DB2 pureScale cluster scaling from 1 to 128 members—without any application changes—for a web commerce workload*

The workload we used for this test was a web commerce application, which was characterized with a 95 percent read and 5 percent write (95R:5W) transaction load, which is typical for this kind of application. As previously mentioned, there was no cluster awareness built into the application. The results of this test are shown in Figure 2.1.

In Figure 2.1, you can see that this architectural proof point started with a single member, and when a second member was dynamically added to the DB2 pureScale cluster, the environment demonstrated 95 percent scalability *without* changing the application. A third member was added, then a fourth, and a fifth; we continually added members to the cluster *without* affinitizing connections, or changing workload, data distribution, and so on, and we observed 95 percent scalability all the way up to 64 members: simply incredible results!

We really wanted to stress the system and go where other clustering software just hasn't been shown to go; therefore (again *without* changing the application or tuning the database), we added more and more members until we got to 128 members, and the DB2 pureScale still demonstrated pretty impressive scalability!

The "Scale-as-You-Would-in-the-Real-World" Test

Okay, perhaps we got a little carried away with the 128-member test, but we think the test in the previous section demonstrates that you can really minimize costly and risky application changes when your host computers are running on DB2 pureScale and you need more capacity. Of course, let's not forget that added capacity can be purchased on a per-day basis, which makes you truly appreciate how special an opportunity you have to really change the way things are done—for the better—with DB2 pureScale.

In our "closer to home" test, we wanted to highlight DB2 pureScale scaling capabilities with a more challenging transactional application that would represent a more UPDATE-intensive workload. The workload for the test used in Figure 2.2 contained one UPDATE transaction for every four READ transactions (20U:80R). Again, there was *no* cluster-awareness built into the application, no routing of transactions to specific members—it was purely transparent.

The hardware configuration for the DB2 pureScale cluster used to deliver the results in Figure 2.2 included 14 eight-core POWER p550 host computers. Specifically, 12 p6 550 servers were dedicated for the 12 members in the cluster. We wanted this test to emulate the kind of high availability that a typical production environment would require, so we used an additional 2 host computers (one operating as a primary and the other a secondary) for the cluster

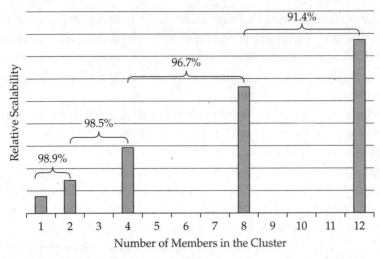

Figure 2.2 *A DB2 pureScale cluster scaling from 1 to 12 members—without any application changes—for a more challenging transactional workload*

caching facility (CF) — sometimes referred to as the PowerHA pureScale server in a POWER-based environment; this made the cluster represent a typical customer configuration for availability.

We think the results shown in Figure 2.2 speak for themselves. A scalability level of 98.5 percent was observed for up to 4 members in this cluster (which is more members than most clusters have in production today); 96.7 percent scalability at 8 members; and 91.4 percent scalability at 12 members in the cluster. Therefore, in this benchmark which showcased a typical OLTP application, the addition of 11 members resulted in about 11 times the throughput—*without* any application changes! The other key thing we want you to take away from Figure 2.2 is that this real world test was done in a scaling manner that reflects your business. There aren't many (if any) applications that are going to be scaled from 1 to 128 members in a single shot. That said, you're likely to be asked to double- or quarter-up your resources every so often and that's exactly what Figure 2.2 shows: incremental scaling capacity.

In closing we want to stress that many vendors *claim* to offer transparent application scaling, but after attending their conferences, or reading fine-print disclosures prompted by Wall Street advertisements, we find that to just not be the case. IBM dubbed DB2 pureScale with the term *pure* because it truly is a pure scaling solution. If you look at other pure technology from the IBM Information Management software brand (namely, pureXML and pureQuery), you'll find a pattern: continued differentiation from the competitive landscape.

Part II

From the Technology Perspective

3

DB2 pureScale Key Concepts: A Primer for the Rest of the Book

So far in this book we've discussed the key benefits that DB2 pureScale (or the IBM pureScale Application System) can instantly deliver to your environment. We've also shown you its amazing transparent scaling capabilities. In this chapter, we want to show you what a DB2 pureScale system looks like from a technology perspective; in subsequent chapters we'll go into how the DB2 pureScale software actually works.

A DB2 pureScale System

In a DB2 pureScale solution, DB2 runs on the *host computers* that make up the cluster. Although we've often used the term "host computer" throughout this book to represent a physical server in a DB2 pureScale cluster, it could be a virtualized operating system image; for example, using LPAR technology on a POWER server. In other words, a physical server could have two host computers on it from a DB2 pureScale perspective. The DB2 software that runs on a host computer is referred to as a *member*, or *DB2 pureScale member*. A DB2 member is just the db2sysc process that you're accustomed to with a "vanilla" DB2 installation (as of DB2 9.5 and later, this process contains all of the agent threads, since DB2 is fully threaded on all platforms). The only difference with DB2 pureScale is that you have multiple db2sysc processes (its threads include services for buffer pools, memory regions, log files, and so on), all accessing the same shared copy of the database over different host computers.

In Figure 3.1 you can see an example of a DB2 pureScale cluster that has four members (which implies that each db2sysc process runs on its own host computer); in addition, we take a closer look at what each member looks like on the right side of this figure, using Member 3 as an example.

In a typical production environment, we recommend one member per host computer. For test and quality assurance (QA) purposes, multiple DB2 members can co-exist together on a single host computer. This is not recommended for production as it does not provide horizontal scalability or optimal high availability for production workloads.

As previously mentioned, DB2 pureScale runs on multiple host computers that can all access the same shared storage copy of the database; therefore, DB2 pureScale is referred to as a *data-sharing* architecture (just like DB2 for z/OS Sysplex), which is well suited for most transactional scaling workloads. Each member has equal access to a shared copy of the database over a storage area

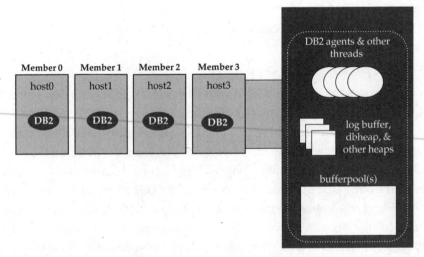

Figure 3.1 *The DB2 pureScale member software running on four physical host computers in a DB2 pureScale cluster*

network (SAN). In addition, each member can write to its own log files as well as access another member's log files (this is very important for availability reasons that we outline in Chapter 6). In Figure 3.2 you see the shared storage added to our example DB2 pureScale environment.

A DB2 pureScale's "nervous system" resides in the *cluster caching facility* (CF). The CF implements global locking services, global buffer management services, and more for a DB2 pureScale cluster; all of this is integral to DB2 pureScale's industry-leading scalability and availability capabilities. (We'll talk about the cluster caching facility software in great detail throughout the remainder of this book.)

NOTE *In a Power-based DB2 pureScale environment, the cluster caching facility is referred to as the PowerHA pureScale server. Since DB2 pureScale is available on other platforms, the term cluster caching facility is used for general DB2 pureScale discussions. If you are working with this technology in a Power-based environment, these terms may sometimes be used interchangeably.*

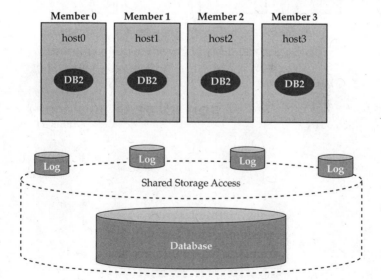

Figure 3.2 *DB2 pureScale operates in a shared-everything architecture and therefore all members have equal access to a shared copy of the database over a SAN.*

In Figure 3.3 you can see there are two cluster caching facility servers: a primary and a secondary. At a high level, the CFs use their memory to manage the state of the DB2 pureScale cluster (they are keeping track of global locks and global buffers, among other things), and most of this information is synchronously kept up to date at both the primary and secondary CF servers. (Although it's not recommended for production environments, you can run a DB2 pureScale cluster with only a single CF; this might be appropriate for certain kinds of test environments.) If a DB2 pureScale cluster loses its primary cluster caching facility services, it can very quickly fail over to the secondary server in a handful of seconds.

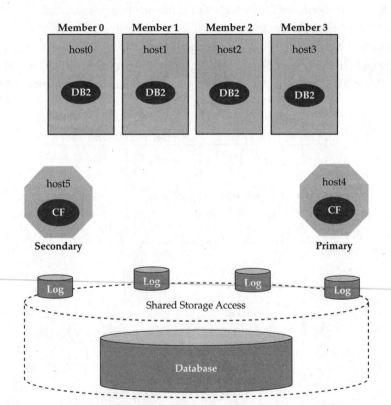

Figure 3.3 *A typical DB2 pureScale solution includes host computers running the DB2 pureScale member software as well as primary and secondary cluster caching facility servers.*

In Figure 3.3 you can see that the primary and secondary CF servers are on their own host computers; however, these resources can be virtualized as well—so you don't have to dedicate a computer for these services. For example, you could have a cluster that consists of two physical computers with each computer running one (or more) members and either the primary or secondary CF software. In short, to have a two-member DB2 pureScale cluster, you *don't need* to have four physically distinct host computers.

There is a high-speed low-latency based data-sharing interconnect, used for all performance sensitive communications, between all of the DB2 pureScale cluster's constituents. DB2 pureScale is achitected to use any RDMA-capable network. InfiniBand was chosen as the initial fabric due to its maturity and wide-use patterns where speed, low latency fabrics are needed. DB2 pureScale was engineered to be a different kind of transaction-optimized technology and therefore uses a special set of instructions that leverage remote direct memory access (RDMA), which in itself is a differentiator compared to most database solutions in the marketplace. What's more, it uses *interrupt-free RDMA* (a differentiating term we want you to remember when it comes to DB2 pureScale) in the processing of RDMA requests. Without getting into details now (we'll talk about this in Chapter 4), there is a lot of "secret sauce" here that really makes DB2 pureScale the heads-and-tails-above solution that it is. As we add in a dedicated high-speed interconnect to our DB2 pureScale example, the environment now looks like Figure 3.4.

DB2 pureScale also includes an integrated component that we refer to as *DB2 Cluster Services* (we cover this in Chapter 6). DB2 Cluster Services is actually a synergistic and enhanced set of three already well-proven IBM software components (and then some) that are fully integrated into DB2 pureScale. DB2 Cluster Services performs the following actions:

- Regulates heart-beats between a cluster's members and the cluster caching facility servers which includes automatically detecting a component failure in the cluster.

- Drives the automation of recovery events that occur when a failure has been detected.

- Handles the clustering and shared access to the shared disk using a clustered file system; this allows the members to access the shared storage through the cluster file system.

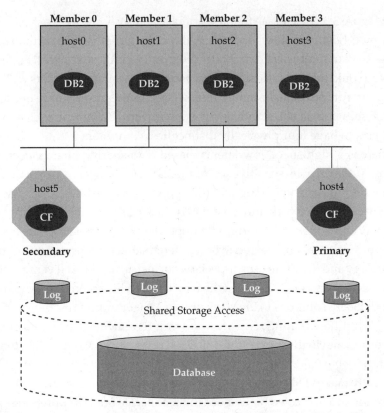

Figure 3.4 *In a DB2 pureScale cluster, members and the central caching facility servers communicate with each other over a high-speed interconnect with interrupt-free RDMA for all performance sensitive communications.*

DB2 Cluster Services (the CS ovals) runs on all the constituents of a DB2 pureScale cluster as shown in Figure 3.5.

The System z and DB2 for z/OS platforms obviously played an enormous role in the creation of DB2 pureScale. In addition, the IBM System Technologies Group (STG) also played a key role in its development. DB2 Cluster Service's heart-beating capabilities come from IBM Reliable Services Clustering Technology (RSCT), which is used in PowerHA SystemMirror (formerly known as HACMP). DB2 pureScale's cluster file system is the IBM General Parallel File System (GPFS)—a highly scalable and reliable file system used in many of today's compute clusters. Of course, as previously mentioned, the cluster caching facility (CF) technology itself has the System z Coupling Facility at its

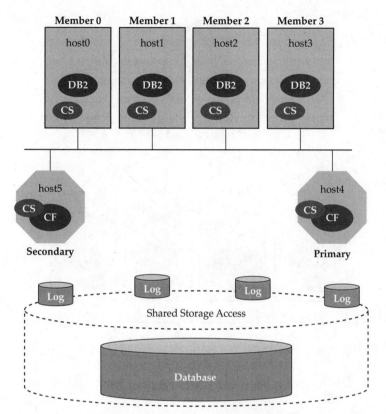

Figure 3.5 *DB2 Cluster Services is part of the DB2 pureScale technology DNA and provides multiple scalability and availability services to the cluster.*

roots. Finally, Tivoli System Automation for Multiplatforms (SA for MP) is at the core of the DB2 pureScale automation capabilities.

As you can see, there are a lot of different IBM components built into this solution, *but* it is one fully integrated solution. When you install DB2 pureScale, all of this code gets laid down for you across all the cluster's host computers; it gets set up and automatically configured for you out of the box (you don't write any failover scripts, and so on); you patch a DB2 pureScale system with a DB2 pureScale Fix Pack—not individual product maintenance, and so on.

To finish off our DB2 pureScale environment example, let's add the clients that connect to the database, as shown in Figure 3.6.

Clients can connect (you can catalog connections to all instance members if you want) to any DB2 pureScale member in the cluster. By default, DB2

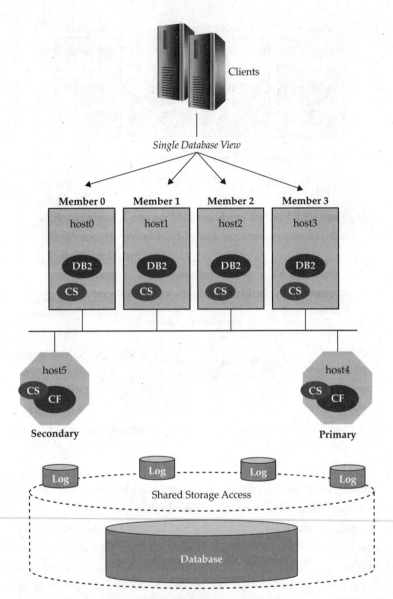

Figure 3.6 *Clients connect to a DB2 pureScale cluster and are transparently workload-balanced across the cluster based on algorithms that understand the cluster's availability and utilization state.*

pureScale will load-balance the work across members of the cluster according to which member is least loaded. For example, an application might connect to Member 1 and issue a transaction against it, but the next incoming transaction (despite connecting to the cluster through Member 1) might get routed to

Member 3 because Member 3 has a lower load than Member 1. If a member were to fail, the work running on it could be transparently rerouted to a surviving member, so the workload balancer algorithm understands the availability of the cluster as well; in addition, you might want to route around a member that you intend to perform maintenance on and DB2 pureScale can handle that scenario too. We talk about the workload-balancing capabilities that are built into DB2 pureScale in Chapter 7.

As you can see, the DB2 pureScale development teams partnered very closely with other divisions in IBM to bring you this solution; we had to in order to truly optimize DB2 pureScale for the task at hand. This optimization isn't marketing veneer; it isn't acquisition and a surface splattering of integration—it is deep integration and optimization from the ground up. The result was industry-leading technology becoming a first-class citizen in DB2 pureScale. For example, you don't have to learn non-database interfaces to manage the cluster or create a clustered file system; we give you DBA-friendly commands (and tooling) for that. What's more, these contributing IBM technologies still exist on their own today, and each has been enhanced in their own right with optimizations and enhancements discovered during the creation of DB2 pureScale.

Now that you have a good understanding of what DB2 pureScale is, how it can scale, and what it looks like, it's time for us to detail the availability and transparent scalability characteristics of this amazing technology.

4

Transparent Application Scaling with DB2 pureScale

A critical property of any cluster database is its ability to scale; that is, its ability to continue delivering strong performance as the workload driving it grows and more compute power is added to the cluster. As a business grows, more and more transactions per second (tps) will naturally need to be processed. If the database systems serving these transactions can't keep up with the increased workload demands, business results will undoubtedly suffer.

The promise of a cluster database is the ability to easily accommodate increased workloads by dynamically and simply adding more compute power to the cluster. The theory is that each computer has equal access to the database, and therefore, the overall cluster can be scaled linearly as more and more computers are added to the cluster to accommodate increased workload demands. Quite simply, if the current requirements of a business were to process 1000 tps, and the business is running on a single host computer, in the future, when the business requirements jump to 2000 tps, the increased load could theoretically be accommodated by simply adding one more computer and creating a cluster. If you doubled the compute resources for a database (in this example, from one host computer to two host computers), and experienced a doubling in the transactions per second achieved by the solution (as in this example, the total processing capability goes from 1000 tps to 2000 tps), this would represent the ideal: *linear scalability*.

In practice, achieving linear scalability for transactional workloads is very difficult to realize for a number of reasons. One such reason has to do with how a clustered database transfers data across its membership. For example, consider a stock trading workload and a respective row that contains the last trade details for some heavily traded stock, such as IBM or Google. As the different host computers within the cluster execute and record transactions corresponding to IBM stock trades, the database page (also known as a block) containing the latest value of this row needs to be transferred back and forth between the host computers in the cluster. This is a very challenging scalability problem for a clustered database to deal with efficiently. Indeed, the effectiveness of a clustered database's ability to efficiently communicate frequently requested data (we refer to this as *hot data*) across different host computers in a cluster usually defines how close to the ideal linear scalability the cluster database will achieve as more and more compute resources are added to it.

In today's marketplace, most cluster database installations have tried to address the hot-data scalability problem themselves by implementing manual partitioning or workload routing in the application itself. For example, if all IBM transactions are routed to host computer 0 in the cluster, and all Google transactions are routed to host computer 1, the need to transfer the corresponding rows between host computers is minimized, and scalability is increased. This approach can work; however, it puts the onus on the IT department supporting the database to intervene and solve the aforementioned scalability challenges, as opposed to the clustered database system itself. This approach to the scalability problem comes at the very high cost of application programming, maintenance, deployment, and a lack of agility. Now consider what happens when more stock symbols are added to the stock trading application. What happens if a single heavily traded stock has a spike of transaction activity due to a strong earnings announcement that overloads the host computer to which that stock's specific transactions are routed? What are the consequences to the application if stock A merges with stock B, or if stock C is split into stock D and stock E? Of course, any of these workload changes can be dealt with by tediously changing the application with more and more custom code; however, such custom programming is difficult, risky, error prone, and very expensive.

A major DB2 pureScale design goal is to minimize (if not eliminate) the need to perform such custom programming, through the use of innovative and highly efficient communication protocols between the host computers. The remainder of this chapter highlights the key aspects of these protocols that make the DB2 pureScale solution so efficient at scaling without having to experience the risks associated with custom application changes, heavily invest in manual and tedious programming, and more.

The DB2 pureScale Scalability "Secret Sauce"

There are three overarching design points that compose the DB2 pureScale communication protocols: *interrupt-less communications, silent invalidation,* and *the cluster caching facility (CF)*—also known as the *PowerHA pureScale server* in POWER-based environments. We like to refer to these techniques and protocols collectively as DB2 pureScale's *secret sauce.*

Interrupt-less Communications

Interrupt-less communications refers to the ability to communicate between host computers without requiring interrupt processing. Normally, host computers within a cluster require interrupts to communicate with any of its constituents. For example, let's consider a cluster with two host computers where Computer A needs to send a message to Computer B. As is often the case, Computer B's processors are all busy executing the transactions that are running on it. Consequently, when the message arrives at Computer B, Computer B's hardware raises an interrupt. This causes the CPU core that has to handle the request on Computer B to store its current execution state in memory, and then suspend the transaction work it was working on in order to *service* the interrupt. The work required to service one of these interrupts could include determining what caused the interrupt, determining what type of message was received, determining which thread on Computer B the message should be delivered to, and so on. Once the interrupt request has been serviced, the CPU core servicing the interrupt can restore the state of the transaction work it was previously running before the interrupt arrived, and resume that work.

However, there are more costs to all these interrupts than what we outlined in the previous paragraph, which creates even more inefficiencies, which impact the scalability of the clustered database. For example, the operating system dispatcher, at some future point in time, will dispatch the thread that the message was meant for to a CPU core so that the thread can actually start processing the message. The CPU cycles consumed performing this interrupt processing can be thought of as overhead as they *are not* directly contributing to the actual processing of the message that was received. These interrupts and their associated processing are extra CPU cycles that are expended just to route the message to the correct target thread. In addition, this interrupt processing can introduce additional subtle inefficiencies known as *cache pollution* (a big problem with transactional workloads), which is the very inefficient act of overwriting cached data relating to the transaction work running on the CPU when the interrupt was received. In addition, once the CPU returns to the transaction, this data must be accessed from slower memory as the CPU switches back to what it was doing (processing the transaction work of the business), as opposed to the fast CPU cache where it resided before all the interrupt processing took place.

In a DB2 pureScale cluster, performance-critical coherency protocols are carried out *without* the need for interrupt processing. The sending thread on Computer A uses a technology known as *Remote Direct Memory Access (RDMA)* to send and receive messages. RDMA allows the communication adapter on Computer A to directly read message data from Computer A's memory, and then sends that data over a communication fabric to the communication adapter on Computer B. Computer B's communication adapter then directly places the data into memory on Computer B, where it can be immediately accessed by threads running on Computer B *without any interrupt processing*. In addition, when a message is expected to be received, DB2 pureScale is designed to keep the receiving thread assigned to a CPU so that it can immediately receive the message data from its memory, without needing to wait for the operating system to dispatch the receiving thread or the introduction of unnecessary cache pollution. For example, a thread making a remote lock request will typically expect the reply to be returned very quickly (we're talking microseconds here), and so will not voluntarily give up its CPU share while the reply is returned.

Silent Invalidation

Another key DB2 pureScale design point relates to how data is kept synchronized across all cluster members in a highly efficient manner. One of the key roles of a clustered database is to provide coherent access to all data, no matter what host computer (*member* in the DB2 pureScale terminology; remember, this entity can be virtualized, so there could be two members on a single computer) a transaction is running on. For example, if a given application executes Transaction 1 on Computer A, and once Transaction 1 completes, it executes Transaction 2 on Computer B (perhaps because Computer B has a lower load), Transaction 2 must be guaranteed to see the results of Transaction 1, just as it would be if it were running against a non-clustered database. Most of today's existing clustered database implementations typically use messaging protocols to accomplish this task. In such technologies, Computer A will send messages to Computer B informing it of Transaction 1's data updates. While this technique does provide the necessary data coherency, it does so in an *inefficient manner* that affects the scalability of the solution. For example, once again (as detailed in the previous section) messages need to be interpreted and processed by Computer B, and this processing requires CPU cycles. Note that we have been using simple illustrations in our scenarios around a two- computer cluster; you can imagine the disproportionate increase in complexities and inefficiencies that get introduced in a larger cluster or as more and more computers are added to a cluster; each additional host computer adds disproportionally more and more inefficiency to the internal operations of most of the clustered database solutions we've seen in the marketplace. Finally, the act of just getting a message to the right thread is a high-overhead operation, as we detailed in the previous discussion on interrupts.

Silent invalidation is a special technique used in DB2 pureScale that informs all cluster members as to the existence of newly committed data in an extremely efficient manner. In fact, this technique requires *no CPU cycles at all* except on the initiating member. Quite simply, this means that if all members of the cluster are performing transactions related to the IBM stock used in this chapter's sample stock-trading application, when Member A completes and commits its transaction (whatever change to the IBM stock was a result of the transaction), all the other members in the DB2 pureScale cluster are instantly informed of the fact that there is new committed data pertaining to the IBM stock *without* any processing cycles being consumed on those other members; this is why we describe this coherency mechanism with the adjective *silent*.

As was the case with interrupt-less communications, RDMA again plays a central role in the silent invalidation implementation as well. For example, before a transaction is allowed to commit in a DB2 pureScale environment, all other participants in the cluster that are buffering data pages that were affected by the most recently processed transaction have their buffered copies *invalidated* via RDMA (remember, no interrupt processing!). Specifically, when a transaction that changes the data is committed, before the commit processing is complete, an RDMA operation sets a validation byte that's associated with each affected page on any member in the DB2 pureScale cluster that is buffering the page in its local buffer pool. This byte is set to a value indicating that the target member's buffered copy of the page is no longer valid (because it was changed). The next attempt to access this now-invalidated page on a member that has an old copy of the data will trigger the member to re-acquire the latest copy of the page such that it is working with the most current version of the data. (As you may have guessed, this re-acquire operation is also implemented using RDMA, so it is efficient.) These RDMA operations are initiated remotely to the target members. On each target member, the communication adapter directly updates its main memory, without requiring host CPU cycles on the target member. As a result, no messages need to be received and/or processed by the target members in order to receive knowledge that their buffered copies of the data are no longer valid and out of date.

Cluster Caching Facility pureScale Technology

The final design point that's a key contributor to the scalability (and transparency of that scalability) associated with a DB2 pureScale cluster is the cluster caching facility (CF) software itself. (When DB2 pureScale was only available on AIX, the CF used to be referred to solely as the PowerHA pureScale server software; today, the CF technology is generally referred to as the CF and in AIX environments often as the PowerHA pureScale server software.) The CF plays a central role in all of DB2 pureScale's communications and coherency operations, including interrupt-less communications and silent invalidation. The CF is specialized software that provides global locking services, group buffer pool services, and several other services; each of these services is optimized for low latency and high efficiency.

The global locking service provided by the CF provides a very low-latency lock service using interrupt-less communications. A member running a transaction that requires some sort of lock (for example, a row or table lock) sends a lock request using RDMA to a CF server. Dedicated threads on the CF server will immediately notice such requests and process them, and once the request is processed, it's replied to—again using RDMA. Since the CF server has threads dedicated for this very purpose, once again, there is no interrupt processing required, which results in DB2 pureScale lock request and reply round-trip times that are typically measured in microseconds.

The group buffer pool service provides a global cache for frequently referenced and recently updated pages. Those hot pages we referred to earlier in this chapter (such as those containing IBM or Google stock trade information) in the cluster will typically find their way into this group buffer pool cache. As such, when a member requests the latest copy of a page with this data, they can be served up to the requesting member very efficiently from the CF via RDMA. The group buffer pool service also contains a page registry, which is the "brains" behind silent invalidation. The CF's page registry records what pages are buffered in each member's local buffer pools. When the group buffer pool receives a new version of a page, the page registry information allows the CF to inform all the members in the DB2 pureScale cluster that have a copy of the page that their copies are invalid and need to be refreshed before they can be transacted upon.

If you have experience with the IBM System z Sysplex, you may have already noticed some similarities between the IBM System z Sysplex Coupling Facility and the CF software. Indeed, the CF shares a number of common design points and direct lineage with the System z Coupling Facility. Many of the same design points that have made the IBM System z Sysplex and the DB2 for z/OS Data Sharing feature the industry gold standard for availability and scalability have been implemented in the CF software that's part of a DB2 pureScale solution.

DB2 pureScale Scalability Technology in Action: A Sample Scenario

Let's walk through a scenario so we can better illustrate how the key DB2 pureScale design points outlined in the previous sections fit together to deliver the DB2 pureScale value proposition. We'll start with a web commerce application workload where the year's most popular product, the blue zapper, is sold to clients all over the world through the Internet. Furthermore, we'll assume that blue zappers are in such hot demand that the Just in Time (JiT) inventory system used to manage them is frequently out of stock. Given the popularity of the blue zapper, it follows that the database page containing the row that indicates their stock level for the JiT system is likely to be frequently accessed on each member in the DB2 pureScale cluster. Furthermore, this data page will also be frequently updated as orders come in and are processed for the blue zapper. Because of the high activity rates on this page, it's also likely that this data page will be cached in each member's local buffer pool and also on the CF. When a blue zapper order comes in, it will be directed to and executed on one of the members in the DB2 pureScale cluster—typically the member with the lowest load (we discuss load balancing in more detail in Chapter 7). When a blue zapper order is committed, the new version of this page containing the resulting stock level updated by this member will be sent to and stored in the group buffer pool in the CF. At the same time, the CF will use its page registry to silently invalidate the copies of the page that are cached on other members in the DB2 pureScale cluster.

Now let's delve into this scenario in a little more detail so that we can illustrate the processing flows that occur in a DB2 pureScale cluster from a transaction perspective. To keep things simple, let's start with a small DB2 pureScale cluster that has two members. In addition, for simplicity, the following figures will only show the interaction between the members and the primary CF server (the secondary CF server is left out of this example—but we cover its importance and use in Chapter 6).

Once the DB2 pureScale cluster is started for our scenario, it would look similar to Figure 4.1.

At the startup time depicted in Figure 4.1, you can see that no data is cached in any of the member's local buffer pools or the global buffer pool (GBP) on the CF server. Of course, at this point all the data is stored on disk, as illustrated by the rectangle within the Database Storage cylinder in Figure 4.1; the data page (rectangle) in the Database Storage cylinder represents the page containing the row with the stock level for blue zappers.

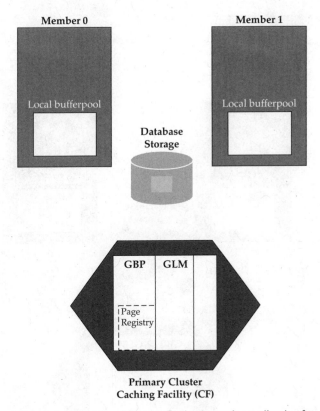

Figure 4.1 *A simple two member DB2 pureScale cluster immediately after startup*

Let's assume now a customer—Adam—is browsing the web site and makes an inquiry about the popular blue zapper (see ❶ in Figure 4.2). The DB2 pureScale load balancer chooses to direct this query to Member 0, which will likely see a SQL statement similar to the following:

```
select STOCK_LEVEL from PRODUCTS where NAME = 'blue zapper'
```

Once Member 0 determines what page number contains the row with blue zapper inventory data, it will attempt to access that page in its local buffer pool. In this case, the page is not yet buffered in Member 0's local buffer pool, so Member 0 will find a free slot in which to store the page, and ask the primary CF server if the page is buffered in the group buffer pool (GBP) by sending it a *Read and Register (RaR)* request (❷). Note that the target page is still not yet buffered in the GBP, so a negative reply is sent to Member 0 (❹). The member responds to the fact that the page it's interested in isn't available in the GBP

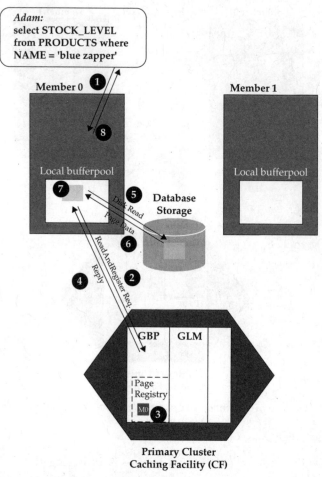

Figure 4.2 *Member 0 reads the stock level of blue zappers.*

and therefore reads the page from disk into its local buffer pool slot it identified earlier (**5** and **6**). It's important to note, however, that the RaR request sent in (**2**) contains all the information that allows the GBP to record the fact that Member 0 is interested in this particular page. Therefore, upon receiving the RaR request, the GBP knows that Member 0 will subsequently read the page from disk, and so it registers Member 0's interest in this page in its page registry (**3**). When these steps have completed, Member 0 will be able to read the stock level from the page in its local buffer pool and return it (**7** and **8**) to the client. The RaR processing is an additional step compared to what you would see in a non-clustered database; however, its performance impact is minimized due to DB2 pureScale's use of interrupt-less RDMA-based communications. In addition, the act of registration doesn't require any extra communications as registration information is *piggy-backed* on the RaR request itself.

At this point, Adam is lucky to find that indeed there are some blue zappers that are still in stock and he decides to purchase one. From a database perspective, this option will result in an update to the row and page containing the stock level for blue zappers through SQL statements that may look similar to the following:

```
update PRODUCTS set STOCK_LEVEL =  STOCK_LEVEL-1 where
NAME = 'blue zapper'
commit
```

Before Adam's purchase transaction is allowed to commit, DB2 pureScale will ensure that this updated page image is cached in the GBP. When the UPDATE SQL statement (step ❶ in Figure 4.3) is processed, Member 0 will modify the page in its local buffer pool (indicated via the now cross-hatched copy of the interested page shown in ❷), and successfully return the UPDATE SQL statement (❸)—note that the transaction isn't committed yet.

At this point, Member 0 remembers that the interested page is *dirty* and, at some future and convenient point in time, uses RDMA to write it to memory into the GBP. Later, when the commit SQL statement is received from Adam's purchase transaction (❻), Member 0 will ensure that this RDMA operation has already completed, and if not, completes it at this time (❹ and ❺). When the RDMA operation is confirmed complete, indicating that the GBP now has the new version of the page, the commit SQL statement returns successfully (❼).

At this point, our astute readers may note that storing this updated page in the GBP is an operation not performed in a non-clustered database. It's done in DB2 pureScale for two key reasons. First, any future reference to this page from another member can be efficiently serviced from the GBP (making it faster at getting this data than if it had to go to even an SSD drive), because as described previously, the CF has dedicated threads that can respond to such requests through RDMA and interrupt-less communications. This can significantly improve performance because the other members don't need to perform storage I/O operations to read the same page data, and do not need to go through an intermediary (sometimes referred to as a master node) to determine where the latest copy of the page data is. Second, storing the latest

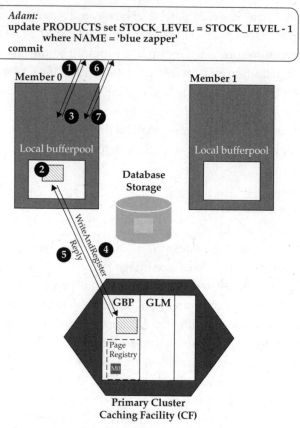

Figure 4.3 *Member 0 updates the stock level of blue zappers.*

committed data values in the GBP significantly improves the performance of the automated recoveries that will occur in the event of a failure. We will discuss this in more detail in Chapter 6.

Now, let's suppose that another customer—Katie—is also interested in the now-infamous blue zapper. As she browses the product on the web, the following SQL statement is executed:

```
select STOCK_LEVEL from PRODUCTS where NAME = 'blue zapper'
```

If you look at Figure 4.4, you'll note that Katie's transaction happens to be load-balanced to execute on Member 1.

Figure 4.4 shows the pertinent steps performed by Member 1 during the processing of this SQL statement. The steps taken here are similar to those that Member 0 performed, when Adam browsed the stock level for blue zappers

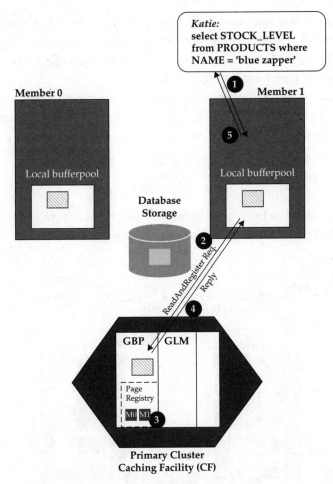

Figure 4.4 *Member 1 reads the stock level of blue zappers.*

depicted in Figure 4.2. Note here, however, that even though Member 1's buffer pool is empty, it does not need to issue a database storage I/O operation to read the page. Instead, it will read the latest committed version of the page from the CF server's GBP, using RDMA (**2** and **4**). This demonstrates some of the advantages of the GBP as it is important not only to avoid the I/O operation, but also to ensure transaction correctness and integrity. After all, Katie may not be pleased if she sees the item in stock, and then decides to order it expecting immediate delivery, only to find later that the item is back-ordered. Member 1 obtains the latest committed version of the page through the RaR

RDMA request and response. In this case, the response will return the page data to Member 1. Note also that Member 1's interest in this page is recorded in the GBP, during the processing of the RaR RDMA request (❸), just as Member 0's interest was registered, in Figure 4.2.

Let's expand our scenario and assume Katie decides to purchase the blue zapper; as she checks out her shopping cart the following SQL statements are issued by the web facing application on her behalf:

```
update PRODUCTS set STOCK_LEVEL =  STOCK_LEVEL-1
     where NAME = 'blue zapper'
commit
```

The steps Member 1 performs here are similar to those performed by Member 0 in Figure 4.3, and they are shown in Figure 4.5.

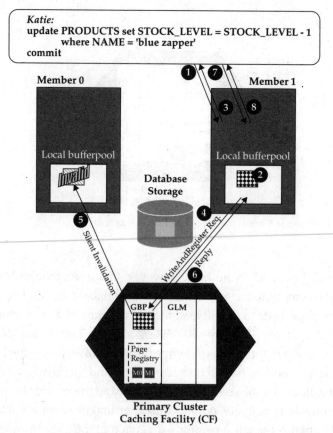

Figure 4.5 *Member 1 updates the stock level of blue zappers.*

When the UPDATE SQL statement (**1**) is processed, Member 1 will modify the page in its local buffer pool indicated via the diamond fill on the page by (**2**), and return the UPDATE SQL statement successfully (**3**). Member 1 will then remember that this page is dirty and, at some future and convenient point in time, use RDMA to write it to memory in the GBP. Later, when the commit SQL statement is received from Katie's purchase transaction (**7**), Member 1 will ensure that this RDMA operation has already completed, or if not, complete it at this time (**4**, **5**, and **6**).

Notice the RDMA-based silent invalidation (**5**) in the previous figure. It's required at this point because unlike the scenario illustrated in Figure 4.2, another member (in this case Member 0) is currently caching a previous version of the page depicted here in Figure 4.5. Specifically, Member 0 is registered in the GBP as having an interest in (for example, a cached copy of) this target page. Member 0 therefore needs to be made aware of the existence of the new version of the data before that new data is committed by Member 1. When the CF sees the new version of the page (**4**), it will use RDMA to reach out to the address space in Member 0, and update the validation byte associated with Member 0's copy of the page in its local buffer pool, indicating to Member 0 that this copy of the page is now invalid.

Once this silent invalidation is complete and visible to any thread running on Member 0, the COMMIT SQL statement may complete successfully (**8**) on Member 1. Again, the key thing to note here is that the silent invalidation is indeed silent with respect to Member 0. That is, no host CPU cycles are required on Member 0 to invalidate the cached page. This becomes increasingly important as the cluster grows—especially when frequently referenced pages are cached in multiple members' buffer pools, as often occurs with database workloads. In these situations, when any of these pages are updated and committed, the number of CPU cycles required on those other members for them to be aware of the existence of the newly committed data *remains at zero*, regardless of cluster size. In contrast to this, other clustered database implementations that use messaging techniques likely incur a significantly increased cost as the cluster grows.

Let's add one more churn in our scenario and illustrate what happens if another customer inquires about blue zappers on Member 0; specifically, Theresa has developed a fond interest in the blue zappers product, and her inquiry into their stock levels is transparently routed to Member 0 as shown in Figure 4.6.

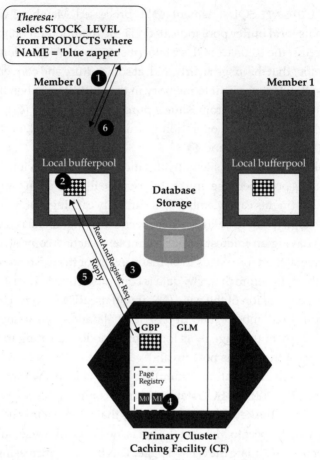

Figure 4.6 *Member 0 again reads the stock level of blue zappers.*

As shown in Figure 4.6, Member 0 benefits from the caching taking place in the GBP, as Member 1 did previously in Figure 4.4. It can acquire the latest version of the page via RDMA from the CF, without performing a database storage I/O. When performing the query, it will look up the target page in its local buffer pool. Normally, it would simply read the row data from this copy of the page. However, in this case, the page is marked invalid (❷) and this will trigger Member 0 to request the latest version of the page from the CF (❸). As we've seen in the previous scenarios, this will create a page registration (❹), before the page image is returned (❺) to Member 0, and the data is returned as the result set of the SELECT statement (❻).

DB2 pureScale Scalability—
A Summary and More

It's so critical to understand the key tenets that contribute to the transparent scalability capabilities of a DB2 pureScale solution that we thought we would summarize the scalability optimizations discussed and illustrated here to conclude this chapter.

There are four key things we want you to remember about the DB2 pureScale technology from a scalability perspective:

- There are two levels of page caching. The first level is the usual buffer pool cache (a member's local buffer pool) in DB2 pureScale. The second level of caching is the group buffer pool located on the CF which caches frequently referenced and updated pages.

- When a new version of a page is in the process of being committed, knowledge of this new version is propagated to all members that are caching an older version of the page through a technique called silent invalidation. Silent invalidation requires no CPU cycles on the other DB2 pureScale cluster members, regardless of the size of the cluster.

- Pages in the GBP are delivered to members that need the latest version of those pages, through interrupt-less RDMA, without storage I/O operations, or any involvement from an intermediary node.

- All performance-sensitive communications are performed through efficient RDMA-based, interrupt-less communications.

In this chapter we concentrated on the page buffering and coherency protocols. These protocols are typically the most important contributors to performance and scalability in a DB2 pureScale cluster database; however, they are certainly not the only key performance and scalability optimizations we've delivered in the DB2 pureScale technology. Other notable techniques used include the following:

- **Low latency lock acquisition** Whenever a member needs to globally lock an object (for example, a table or a row), that request will be sent (via RDMA) to the CF's global lock manager (GLM). What's more, a dedicated thread at the GLM will notice the request appear in the CF server's memory, process it, and send the response (once again, this is all done with interrupt-free RDMA). The member thread that sent the request will then notice that the reply is present in its memory, and proceed. The use of RDMA and dedicated threads in this manner allows interrupt-less communications, and round-trip lock latencies that are measured in microseconds.

- **Lock prefetching and batching**   There are instances during execution where, on a non-clustered database system, a DB2 thread running a transaction may acquire and/or release different locks sequentially, one after another. In DB2 pureScale, many of these instances have been restructured to perform all the locking-related activities within a single interaction with the GLM. For example, when a transaction ends, all locks may be released in a single batch (as opposed to separate lock release requests to the GLM). This technique further reduces the after-latency per-lock operation.

- **Asynchronous lock operations**   There are occasions where a lock operation may be initiated, and before it completes, transaction work may proceed. Lock release is one example of such an occasion. Confirmation that the lock has been released is usually not necessary for a transaction to continue its work. DB2 pureScale exploits this optimization in certain locations, further driving down the average latency per lock operation.

- **Lock avoidance**   Despite the optimizations listed so far, which result in a very low average latency per lock operation, it's even better for a database to avoid locks altogether when possible (assuming they aren't needed). DB2 pureScale exploits cursor stability (CS)-based currently commited locking semantics to avoid taking locks in many common cases. Although this topic is outside the scope of this book, this is also a benefit for non-clustered DB2 databases as of DB2 9.7.

- **Table append cache and index page cache**   What happens in the case of rapid concurrent `INSERT` operations into the same single table by multiple members? Will it cause the target page to be sent back and forth between the members, each time a member has a new row to insert? No! Each member sets aside a set of pages (termed an *append cache*) for insertion into the table to eliminate contention and page thrashing. An analogous page cache is used for index updates.

- **Concurrent page access**   In a non-clustered system, a page being updated by one transaction is not concurrently readable by another transaction. If the other transaction attempted to read the page while it was being updated by the first transaction, the other transaction may see partially updated data, and results would likely be incorrect. In DB2 pureScale, because each member has its own local buffer pool, a transaction running on Member 0 can read a page at the same precise instant that a different transaction, running on Member 1, is updating the page (under most isolation levels).

This chapter provided you with a summary of DB2 pureScale's *secret sauce*—specifically, a summary of the design points used to provide strong performance and scalability characteristics as the cluster grows, without the need for expensive and difficult application redesign. Another important cluster database topic is availability: maintaining service despite a computer failure, for example. Chapter 6 focuses on the design points DB2 pureScale uses to maximize overall system availability.

5

DB2 pureScale Configuration: The Operational 101

In this chapter we'll introduce you to some of the basic day-to-day configuration knowledge that you will need for any DB2 pureScale environment. It's obviously outside the scope of this book to delve into deep details, but the information contained in this chapter should give you enough to have a basic understanding of how a DB2 pureScale environment is configured, and the basic tasks you should know how to perform as a database administrator (DBA) assigned to managing such an environment.

A DB2 pureScale Instance

A DB2 pureScale instance consists of DB2 members and the cluster caching facility (CF) servers (also known as the *PowerHA pureScale servers* in a POWER-based environment) that all run on *host computers*. A host computer refers to a physical computer running an operating system in either a traditional manner (one operating system per computer) or a virtualized manner (for example, you could have two distinct LPARs running two distinct AIX operating systems on the same physical piece of hardware). In this chapter, for simplicity, we might refer to host computers as *hosts*, but the term *computers* can be used synonymously with it as well. A DB2 *member* is a software server comprised of a set of processes (for example, db2sysc, db2wdog, and more).

The CF is also comprised of a set of processes (for example, `ca-server`, `ca-wdog`, and more).

Any DB2 pureScale instance must have at least one DB2 pureScale member and one CF server. A typical production-ready DB2 pureScale environment will have at least two DB2 members (to provide scalability and active-active high availability) and two CF servers (to eliminate a single point of failure).

The host computers involved in a DB2 pureScale instance, and the designation of which host computers run the CF server software versus which host computers run the DB2 pureScale member software, is specified at deployment time through the installation program. Alternatively, you can install the DB2 pureScale code and designate what host computers run the CF server software and which ones run the DB2 pureScale member software as part of the manual creation of a DB2 pureScale instance after a basic installation.

Figure 5.1 shows a sample DB2 pureScale environment that has four DB2 pureScale members and two CF servers. As you can see in Figure 5.1, this DB2 pureScale cluster has been instantiated on six host computers (the first is `host0` and the last is `host5`). Of those, `host0`, `host1`, `host2`, and `host3` are running the DB2 pureScale member software while `host4` and `host5` are running the CF server software.

DB2 pureScale Configuration: The db2nodes.cfg File

The *db2nodes.cfg* file explicitly lists all of the host computers that the DB2 pureScale members and CF servers are designated to run on in the cluster. An example of a *db2nodes.cfg* file for the DB2 pureScale cluster shown in Figure 5.1 is shown in the following code:

```
db2nodes.cfg
0     host0 0     host0-ib0     MEMBER
1     host1 0     host1-ib0     MEMBER
2     host2 0     host2-ib0     MEMBER
3     host3 0     host3-ib0     MEMBER
4     host4 0     host4-ib0     CF
5     host5 0     host5-ib0     CF
```

The first, second, fourth and last columns are the most important entries to understand in this file. Each line in the *db2nodes.cfg* refers to a DB2 pureScale member or CF server in the instance. The first column indicates the ID of the

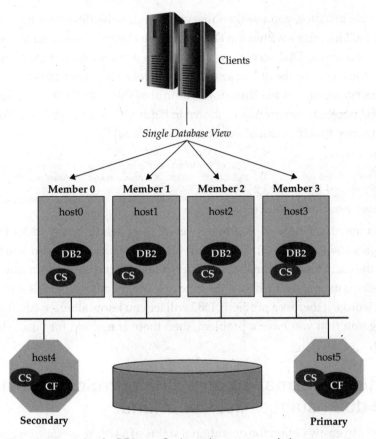

Figure 5.1 *An example of a DB2 pureScale environment on six host computers*

member or CF server in the DB2 pureScale cluster. The second column lists the hostname of the host computer that the member or CF server associated with the ID is designated to run on. The fourth column lists the name of the adapter to be used for data sharing communications on the host computer. Finally, the last column designates the entry in the *db2nodes.cfg* as a DB2 pureScale member or CF server. Note that a *db2nodes.cfg* file could have two lines listing the same host computer as multiple members (or a combination of member and CF server software) could be running in the same physical computer.

Starting a DB2 pureScale Cluster

If you've used DB2 before, it's likely that you are already familiar with the db2start command that's used to start a DB2 instance. To start a DB2 pureScale instance, you use the same command, only the output includes all of the DB2 members within the DB2 pureScale cluster as opposed to the start status of a single DB2 server, as is the case in a non-clustered DB2 environment. You can issue the db2start command for a DB2 pureScale cluster from any host computer in the cluster. The output of the db2start command for the DB2 pureScale environment shown in Figure 5.1 is shown in the following code (notice that the cluster was started on host0):

```
host0> db2start
08/24/2008 00:52:59  0  0   SQL1063N  DB2START processing was successful.
08/24/2008 00:53:00  1  0   SQL1063N  DB2START processing was successful.
08/24/2008 00:53:01  2  0   SQL1063N  DB2START processing was successful.
08/24/2008 00:53:01  3  0   SQL1063N  DB2START processing was successful.
SQL1063N  DB2START processing was successful.
```

You may have noticed that there weren't any results returned for the CF servers, (ID=4 and ID=5). The CF servers *are automatically started* when you issue the db2start command; however, if these servers start normally, there is no status message returned, unlike the case of a member when it's started. In other words, if there is a problem, DB2 will let you know about it; and if it isn't telling you that you have a problem, then there is nothing for you to worry about.

Getting Information on a DB2 pureScale Cluster: The db2instance –list Command

A DBA can easily obtain the operational status of a DB2 pureScale instance by issuing the db2instance –list command. The output of running this command (issued from the host computer associated with ID=0) for the DB2 pureScale environment shown in Figure 5.1 is shown in the following code:

```
host0> db2instance -list

ID TYPE     STATE      HOME_HOST  CURRENT_HOST ALERT
0  MEMBER   STARTED    host0      host0        NO
1  MEMBER   STARTED    host1      host1        NO
2  MEMBER   STARTED    host2      host2        NO
3  MEMBER   STARTED    host3      host3        NO
4  CF       PRIMARY    host4      host4        NO
5  CF       PEER       host5      host5        NO

HOST_NAME  STATE      INSTANCE_STOPPED    ALERT
host0      ACTIVE     NO                  NO
host1      ACTIVE     NO                  NO
host2      ACTIVE     NO                  NO
```

```
host3      ACTIVE      NO                  NO
host4      ACTIVE      NO                  NO
host5      ACTIVE      NO                  NO
```

You can see that the output of the db2instance -list command is divided into two sections. The first section returns information about the members and the CF servers from a software perspective.

The first column of the first section includes the now familiar ID field, which corresponds to the ID of the specific member or CF server as defined in the *db2nodes.cfg* file.

The TYPE column identifies whether the ID is associated with a DB2 member (TYPE=MEMBER) or a CF server (TYPE=CF). In the above example db2instance -list output, you can see that all of the members defined for this DB2 pureScale cluster have STATE=STARTED, indicating that db2start processing was successful and the DB2 pureScale member software is working normally. You can also see that ID=4 and ID=5 are CF servers (since their TYPE=CF). For the CF servers, instead of the STATE field denoting its status with respect to its start state, the output relays information that pertains to the role this particular CF is performing in the instance. You can see in the previous example that the CF associated with ID=4, whose STATE=PRIMARY, is operating as the primary CF server. If STATE=PEER, then the CF is acting as the backup (sometimes referred to as secondary, as is the case in Figure 5.1) CF server. A CF server that is operating in PEER state is ready to assume primary responsibilities for the cluster's lock management services, global buffer pool services, and other CF-supported services should a failure occur. In the running example used in this chapter, if a failure occurs on host4, then the CF ID=5, running on host5, would take over the primary CF responsibilities. As you've likely figured out, a STATE of PRIMARY or PEER indicates that the CF server software is running just fine on their respective host computers.

The HOME_HOST field designates the host computer that the member or CF server software is designated to run on when everything in the cluster is running just fine. In contrast, the CURRENT_HOST field designates where the respective DB2 pureScale member is currently running. For example, let's assume the output of the db2instance- list command had the following entries:

```
. . .
1  MEMBER   STARTED   host1     host1     NO
2  MEMBER   STARTED   host2     host1     NO
. . .
```

Notice how the member associated with ID=2 has HOME_HOST=host2 but CURRENT_HOST=host1? We can conclude in this scenario that a failure occurred on the host computer for the member ID=2 and that member has been relocated to a different host computer (in this case, host1) for recovery.

Finally, the ALERT field indicates if manual intervention is required to restore the failed software to a normal operating state. For example, if a member was to fail, but the failure was recoverable without DBA intervention, this field would still be set to NO. Quite simply, if you see this field set to YES, it means you (or someone) has to get involved to manually rectify the problem.

The second part of the db2instance -list command returns information as it relates to the host computers (remember, they could be LPARs) in the DB2 pureScale instance and their associated state. The HOST_NAME field, as its name indicates, gives you the host name of the host computer. The STATE refers to the operational state of the host computer itself. In this case, STATE=ACTIVE means that the associated host computer is operating normally. The INSTANCE_STOPPED field indicates whether a db2stop instance on host <hostname> command has been issued against a specific host computer in the cluster; for example, you might issue this command to perform planned maintenance (such as applying an operating system fix) on a specific host computer. In this example, since INSTANCE_STOPPED=NO, no such maintenance activity that would require stopping the instance software running on a specific host computer has been invoked on the DB2 pureScale cluster. Finally, the ALERT field operates in the same manner as the corresponding field in the first section of this command's output; namely, it will be set to YES only if manual intervention is required on the host computer itself to rectify the problem.

We will delve into more details about scenarios where the HOME_HOST and CURRENT_HOST fields are not the same, or where ALERT=YES, and how to resolve them in Chapter 6.

Provisioning Storage for a DB2 pureScale Instance

DB2 pureScale requires shared storage that is accessible as small computer system interface (SCSI) logical unit numbers (LUNs) to each host computer in the DB2 pureScale cluster. Such storage will typically be connected to the cluster either through a storage area network (SAN) or by directly attaching storage controllers to host computers in the cluster.

When you install and configure a DB2 pureScale cluster, the installation program will ask you to provision two storage devices for a pureScale instance as shown in Figure 5.2.

The installation program uses the paths you specify in Figure 5.2 to set up and configure the file system capabilities associated with DB2 Cluster Services which helps provide high-availability services to a DB2 pureScale environment. We'll discuss DB2 Cluster Services in detail in Chapter 6.

The first shared LUN specified in Figure 5.2 is used to create a cluster file system that stores instance metadata that is shared across members in a directory called *sqllib_shared*. If you have DB2 experience, you're no doubt familiar with the ubiquitous *sqllib* directory that's created during any DB2 installation in the instance owner's path (in UNIX and Linux deployments; on Windows, this directory is located in the standard *Program Files/IBM* directory). In a DB2 pureScale environment, members share the directory called *sqllib_shared* so the instance metadata can be shared across the cluster. DB2 pureScale instances also have a *sqllib* directory (in the instance owner's *home* directory) on each host computer; however, unlike the *sqllib_shared* directory, *sqllib* is a local directory that every DB2 member has, and not a single shared directory like *sqllib_shared*.

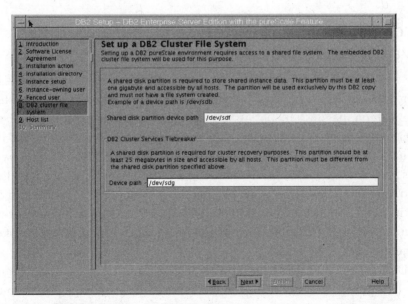

Figure 5.2 *The DB2 pureScale installation program prompting you to define the storage devices used in the cluster*

The second shared LUN specified in Figure 5.2 is used as a tie-breaker de-vice and does not need to be particularly large in size. It is used by DB2 Cluster Services as a tie-breaking vote in the event that half of the host computers in a DB2 pureScale instance fail. A DB2 pureScale instance requires 1/2 + 1 votes for the instance to function. This concept is known as *operational quorum*. Oper-ational quorum is needed to prevent a pathological condition known as *split-brain*, which will be discussed in Chapter 6. Each host computer in a DB2 pureScale instance has one quorum vote. An additional vote can be obtained by DB2 Cluster Services' quorum algorithm by virtue of an exclusive SCSI lock on the specified tie-breaker disk. The presence of a tie-breaking vote al-lows an instance to continue running even if half of the host computers were to fail. For example, in a four-host computer instance, if two out of the four host computers suffered a catastrophic hardware failure, the DB2 pureScale in-stance would continue to operate because the two surviving host computers would provide one quorum vote each to DB2 Cluster Services, and DB2 Clus-ter Services would be able to obtain an additional vote by locking the tie-breaker disk. Since three votes will ultimately be obtained by DB2 Cluster Services, and three is a majority in a four-host computer instance, the instance will have operational quorum and will continue to function normally through the two surviving host computers.

Provisioning Storage for a Database in a DB2 pureScale Instance

We recommend that you create two separate file systems for each DB2 pureScale database: one for table space containers (for example, used as a stor-age path on the CREATE DATABASE statement), and the other for database logs and metadata. The number of LUNs used for these file systems, and the actual number of spindles backing each LUN, is a topic outside the scope of this book as it is not specifically related to DB2 pureScale; however, with that said, care should be taken to ensure that there is enough I/O bandwidth ca-pacity in the storage tier to sustain the I/O rates that a typical online transac-tion processing (OLTP)–like or enterprise resource planning (ERP)–like system generates.

Once the shared LUNs have been made visible to all the host computers in the DB2 pureScale cluster, DB2 Cluster Services makes storage provisioning straightforward for the DBA tasked with managing the environment. For example, a system administrator isn't required to create a cluster file system; in fact, a system administrator need only change the ownership of the LUNs to the database instance owner ID and then doesn't really need to be involved in the DB2 pureScale cluster's day-to-day operations.

For example, consider the following system where four LUNs (sda1, sda2, sda3, and sda4) were provisioned to a DB2 pureScale project by a storage administrator. Let's further assume that the system administrator changed the ownership of the devices to db2inst1 (assuming this is the DB2 instance owner's ID). You could verify this as shown in the code listing below:

```
myhost:/home/db2inst1> ls -l /dev/sda*
brw-r----- 1 db2inst1 dbag  8,  1 2009-10-07 14:02 /dev/sda1
brw-r----- 1 db2inst1 dbag  8,  2 2009-10-07 14:01 /dev/sda2
brw-r----- 1 db2inst1 dbag  8,  3 2009-10-07 14:02 /dev/sda3
brw-r----- 1 db2inst1 dbag  8,  3 2009-10-07 14:02 /dev/sda4
```

At this point, the DBA could create the two file systems (one as a storage path for the database and the other for database logs and metadata) through the DB2 Cluster Services' db2cluster command as shown in the following code:

```
myhost:/home/db2inst1>
      db2cluster -cfs -create -filesystem datafs -disk
/dev/sda1 /dev/sda2 /dev/sda3 -mount /db2/data

myhost:/home/db2inst1>
      db2cluster -cfs -create -filesystem logfs -disk
/dev/sda4 -mount /db2/logs
```

The two clustered file systems created in the previous example, datafs and logfs, are accessible from all host computers that make up the DB2 pureScale instance. The db2cluster -cfs -create commands don't just create the aforementioned respective file systems; they also mount these file systems on all the host computers in the DB2 pureScale instance, as shown in Figure 5.3.

At this point, a DBA could create the database using the newly created file systems with a command similar to the following:

```
db2 create database mydb ON /db2/data DBPATH ON /db2/logs
```

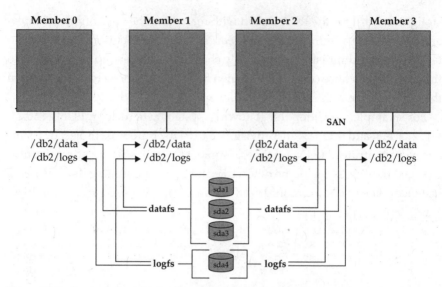

Figure 5.3 *Storage provisioning in a DB2 pureScale instance.*

The db2cluster command allows the DBA to add or remove disks from a file system, and even rebalance a file system to re-stripe (which is done by the cluster file system) the data as shown in the code below:

```
myhost:/home/db2inst1>
db2cluster -cfs -add -filesystem datafs -disk /dev/sda5

myhost:/home/db2inst1>
      db2cluster -cfs -rebalance -filesystem datafs

myhost:/home/db2inst1>
db2cluster -cfs -remove -filesystem datafs -disk /dev/sda3
```

6

DB2 pureScale for Availability

In this chapter we'll talk about the key DB2 pureScale services and features that provide some pretty amazing availability characteristics for your DB2 pureScale cluster. From services that automate the handling of both hardware and software failures, to unprecedented failure detection times, to the most availability of any database (to the best of our knowledge) during recovery operations, and more, DB2 pureScale raises the bar when it comes to providing availability to your transactional environments. In fact, we'll start this chapter out (and likely repeat it because it's music to everyone's ears) by noting that *every DB2 pureScale instance is resilient to software and hardware failures right out of the box.*

Cluster Caching Facility Server Redundancy

While a DB2 pureScale instance can function with a single cluster caching facility (CF) server (sometimes referred to as the PowerHA pureScale server in POWER-based DB2 pureScale environments), we strongly recommend that production instances use two CF servers for redundancy and to eliminate single points of failure within the cluster.

In a typical two-server CF production environment, one CF server assumes the *primary* role and the other a *secondary* role. The secondary CF server is kept synchronously up to date with the primary such that if a failure of the primary CF server were to occur, the application experience would not be impacted, as the services provided by this now failed server would seamlessly failover to the secondary server, which would assume primary responsibility for these services. What's more, during periods of normal operation, the group buffer pool (GBP) and shared communication area (SCA) memory services are fully duplexed between the primary and the secondary CF servers. For example, if the database instance needed to write a page to the GBP as part of a transaction (let's assume the application requested a COMMIT operation), the DB2 pureScale *Force at Commit* protocol would not consider this operation complete until commit information was successfully written to both the primary and secondary CF servers. Remember, a write in this context implies that any page transfers between a DB2 pureScale member and the CF server occur via interrupt-free remote direct memory access (RDMA), as we discussed in Chapter 4.

On the other hand, locks are only partially duplexed between the CF servers. Locks that have been granted by the primary CF's global lock manager (GLM) service to the DB2 pureScale members can be broadly defined as *retained* or *non-retained*. Retained locks are held by the GLM on behalf of a failed DB2 member until its recovery process is complete; once this has happened, the retained locks are freed by the respective DB2 member. Non-retained locks are freed by the GLM as soon as it receives notification that the DB2 member that held them has failed. Broadly speaking, write locks (such as an X lock on a record) are retained, while read locks (such as an S lock on a record) are non-retained. With respect to the partial duplexing of lock information mentioned at the start of this paragraph, only retained locks are duplexed to the secondary CF server. Therefore, if the primary CF server were to fail, the DB2 pureScale members participating in the instance would be requested to send their local lock information to the secondary CF server's GLM such that this secondary server gains a complete view of the cluster's lock states, which are required before the secondary server can be promoted to the primary role.

DB2 Cluster Services

One of the most compelling value propositions around DB2 pureScale is that it comes configured for high availability right out of the box! In fact, a set of subcomponents and services, collectively known as DB2 Cluster Services, build high availability into DB2 pureScale's DNA by providing a set of services that include built-in failure detection, recovery automation, and a cluster file system for shared access of table space containers, logs, and other metadata.

DB2 Cluster Services includes other industry-leading IBM software products such as Tivoli Systems Automation for Multi Platforms (SA for MP), IBM's Reliable Services Clustering Technology (RSCT), and the IBM General Parallel File System (GPFS). One point of clarification is worthy at this point: All of the components that make up DB2 Cluster Services have been tightly coupled together within the DB2 pureScale database engine. In other words, as a DB2 pureScale DBA, you aren't working with three or four different products and maintenance streams, and you're not having to learn the command interfaces for multiple products; rather, all of the subcomponents that make up DB2 Cluster Services are first-class citizens of the database. For example, upgrades and maintenance (such as Fix Packs) to any DB2 Cluster Services components are provided as part of the DB2 pureScale service stream. Unlike traditional cluster managers, DB2 Cluster Services is designed to interact with the database administrator (DBA) through DB2 commands and SQL.

As previously mentioned, every DB2 pureScale instance is automatically configured for high availability and automated recovery right out of the box: It's all part of the creation of a DB2 pureScale instance. In fact, high availability is such an integral part of the DB2 pureScale DNA that you don't even have an option to not have recovery automation setup and configured for you at instance creation time. This is great news for DBAs because it means they don't have to run tedious commands, create cluster management failover policies, write failover scripts, and more to get to a highly available environment.

DB2 Cluster Services continually monitors a DB2 pureScale cluster's members and CF servers to ensure they are healthy after instance startup. In addition, DB2 Cluster Services also monitors other key infrastructure components such as Host Channel Adapters (HCAs), file system access (and therefore implicitly any Host Bus Adapters), the actual host computers themselves, and more. DB2 Cluster Services automatically initiates recovery processing if any of the aforementioned resources are found to be "unhealthy." These recovery operations are coordinated such that they ensure minimal impact to database availability.

Monitoring the Health of DB2 pureScale Cluster Resources

Once a DB2 pureScale instance is started, DB2 Cluster Services automatically monitors the health of cluster resources, which are required to maintain the availability of the cluster to service application transactions. Specifically, some of the resources that DB2 Cluster Services monitors include the following:

- DB2 processes (for example, `db2sysc`, `db2wdog`)
- Cluster caching facility server processes (for example, `ca-server`)
- Host computers in the cluster
- Network adapters (for example, the Host Channel Adapter)
- Access to paths and file systems that are being used by a DB2 pureScale cluster (for example, storage path, log path, and so on)

If any of these resources should fail, DB2 Cluster Services will automatically coordinate the appropriate recovery actions to maintain availability of the database. In fact, DB2 Cluster Services understands the implicit dependencies between all of the aforementioned resources in the DB2 pureScale cluster. For example, one of the cluster's host computers might appear healthy because it's responding to and sending heart-beat messages across the cluster. However, let's assume that the HCA has failed, or perhaps there's a broken link between the adapter and network switch. In such a situation, simply heart-beating wouldn't alert most database software that there is a problem in the cluster. In contrast, DB2 Cluster Services understands that such a host computer is not healthy enough to run DB2 pureScale (the member or CF server software). A DB2 pureScale member or CF that was running on such a host computer at the time that the HCA failure occurred would be stopped automatically by DB2 Cluster Services, and recovery actions (detailed later in this chapter) would be initiated.

DB2 pureScale Member Crash Recovery

To keep things simple, we'll note that there are really two kinds of failures possible in a DB2 pureScale cluster: a DB2 member failure and a CF server failure (we are assuming that anything in between, such as an HCA failure or an HCA link failure, would fall into one of these categories as well).

The failure of one or more DB2 members will result in DB2 Cluster Services driving Member Crash Recovery (MCR). MCR involves log-based REDO and UNDO operations using only the transaction log of the member that crashed. (Note that MCR is performed regardless of whether the member failure was software- or hardware-related.)

Each MCR operation is independent of each other in the sense that each MCR only has to perform log-based recovery based on the transaction log of the DB2 member that the MCR is trying to recover. Therefore, if a failure of more than one DB2 member were to occur in the DB2 pureScale cluster, it will result in concurrent MCR processing for *each* member and there will be *no merging* of the transaction logs to complete MCR processing.

While MCR is occurring on a member in the DB2 pureScale cluster, the database remains available and other DB2 members are *unaffected* by the outage. In fact, any transactions running on any other members continue virtually unaffected unless they need a lock that was held by a transaction running on the now-failed member.

While we're trying to stay away from commenting on our competitors (a topic on which much could be written), we'll note that DB2 pureScale has a single location for lock information: the CF server (remember, there is a secondary CF server in case the primary should fail). The competitive technology that we've looked at distributes lock information across their clusters, and this creates a significant amount of overhead and frozen database access (due to lock master redistribution to surviving nodes) should a failure occur in the cluster. Since DB2 pureScale doesn't need to perform a redistribution of lock mastership metadata, *access to the database is never denied during a member failure; only access to the in-flight data that needs to be made consistent.* This is a very important point, so we want you to read that last sentence twice. It's a differentiator and if you peel away the marketing veneer of some of our competitors, you'll find DB2 pureScale is heads and tails above the competition when it comes to the amount of data that's available to transactions during a failure in the cluster. Quite simply, the centralized locking services provided by the CF server to the DB2 pureScale cluster allow the recovery of a failed member to be completely *online*; hence, you'll sometimes hear us refer to the DB2 pureScale recovery operations as *online recovery.*

When a failure occurs, new transactions can be routed to surviving members, existing transactions continue running, and transactions can commit while MCR is ongoing; there is no freeze of the I/O to the database table space containers by surviving members while MCR is in progress, as is the case with competitive offerings.

The differentiating characteristics of DB2 pureScale from a high availability perspective are shown at the bottom of Figure 6.1.

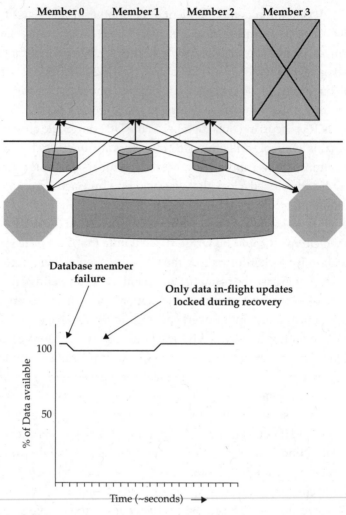

Figure 6.1 *Online recovery*

At the top of Figure 6.1, you can see that a failure has occurred on Member 3 in the example DB2 pureScale cluster (the octagons represent the primary and secondary CF servers). Once such a failure occurs, *only* the data records that were being modified by transactions, but have not yet been committed, remain locked (and therefore inaccessible—as they should be—until they are made transactionally consistent). If you look at the bottom of Figure 6.1, you'll note the data availability graph. You can see in this graph that only a very small amount of data, as a proportion to the total data in the database, is momentarily unavailable. If we were to plot the data availability lines of other vendor databases on this graph, you would find a steep drop (likely between 0 percent and 10 percent) until the master lock information was recovered and redistributed, and then a step-like motion toward full availability; this is a consequence of other shared-everything cluster databases available on Linux, UNIX, and Windows that DB2 pureScale doesn't have to contend with due to its architecture.

Restart Light

Typically, member crash recovery (MCR) for a failed member will occur on a member's home host computer. There are certain failure scenarios, however, where it's possible that the failed member's host computer has either failed, or is not considered healthy enough to perform the member's recovery processing itself. For example, consider a scenario where a member fails due to a hardware issue, so it's not so much the software that caused the failure, but rather the host computer itself that has failed. In this case, MCR processing cannot occur on the member's home host computer (the computer where the now-failed member was running when the DB2 pureScale cluster was running just fine) and the failed member needs to be restarted on another host computer in the cluster.

Restart light is designed to transparently handle this kind of failure in a DB2 pureScale cluster. Restart light is performed using pre-allocated processes which have a very small amount of pre-allocated and pre-pinned memory. These pre-allocated resources are set aside during a healthy state to ensure that compute resources are always available to perform this key availability function, and that it gets to work right away if it's needed as opposed to having to free up compute resources if a problem happens. Think of it as planning for a rainy day. How many times have you wished you had an extra pair of batteries in the car when your kid's DVD headset runs out of battery power? If you have kids, then you know what we are talking about! Specifically, each member's host computer has three db2sysc (idle) processes pre-allocated for this very scenario. When restart light occurs, it takes over a pre-allocated idle db2sysc process and performs MCR using that process and the pre-allocated memory associated with it. Restart light thus ensures that MCR for a member whose host computer is unavailable to perform its own MCR can always be performed very quickly by another host computer since no new process or memory allocation is required. Other examples where restart light will occur are cases where a member's host computer is available, but DB2 Cluster Services detects something unhealthy about it. For example, if a host computer's HCA is down, the member running there will be shut down and restart light will occur.

Restart light will also occur if a DB2 member's MCR on its home host computer is unsuccessful (in this scenario, the failure was software-related as opposed to the previous scenario). If DB2 Cluster Services could not successfully db2start the failed member on its home host computer, an ALERT will be set on that member (we discussed this in Chapter 5) and restart light will be performed. This ensures that if a host computer has some endemic problem—such as a lack of free memory resulting from some runaway non-DB2-related daemon, the member's recovery will not be held up as a result.

If member restart was performed on a guest host computer, when it finished, it will remain on the guest host computer where its recovery was performed and continue to use only a very small memory footprint. In this state, the member (which was once running on its home host computer and has now been successfully restarted on another host computer, referred to as the *guest host computer*) status will be listed as WAITING_FOR_FAILBACK and the member will not be failed back to its home host computer until it's returned to a healthy state. A member, while operating in restart light mode (even after its MCR is done), will not accept connections from applications and thus is not involved in ongoing transaction processing that is occurring within the DB2 pureScale cluster during this time. Note that the member in this scenario stays online as access to its transaction log is required for a potential in-doubt transaction query or resolution attempts that might be performed by a user from a connection to the database on one of the healthy members.

In the specific case of members failing because of a hardware issue (perhaps an HCA issue), DB2 Cluster Services will automatically detect when the HCA has been fixed and is reporting a normal state. Once this happens, the DB2 recovered member that is now running on a guest host computer will transfer back to the home host computer where it was running before the problem arose. On the other hand, if restart light is performed as a result of DB2 Cluster Services being unable to db2start the crashed member on its home host computer, human intervention will be required before the member is failed back to its home host computer. In this case, it's likely that an administrator will have to perform some problem determination (or contact IBM service if necessary) to determine the reason for the db2start failure. Once the failure situation has been addressed, the administrator simply needs to clear the alert on the DB2 member using the db2cluster -cm -clear -alert command. Once the alert on the member is cleared, DB2 Cluster Services will automatically fail the member back to its home host computer.

Member Crash Recovery Performance

After reading the previous section, you've likely realized that the elapsed time measured from when a member crashes to the time that its recovery is completed is critical because retained locks are only freed once MCR is complete. Transactions running on surviving members that need to obtain locks on records that are held locked by the failed member will experience a lock wait during MCR, and such transactions will take longer to complete than they normally would. No question about it; we'll assume that we're all in agreement that minimizing such lock waits is key.

The good news is that DB2 pureScale was designed from the ground up for rapid failure detection and recovery, regardless of the type of failure (hardware or software). From an application's perspective, recovery time includes failure detection time, the steps involved in orchestrating the initiation of recovery, the transaction log REDO and UNDO operations, and finally the freeing of retained locks. Collectively these are all the actions required before the application can successfully resubmit the transaction, which is really what availability means: When can I get back to honoring my service level agreement (SLA)? With that said, we've found lots of vendors in the industry who are marketing recovery times and failing to include things like detection of the failure itself! Some of these detection scenarios can take a number of seconds just to find out there is a problem that needs recovery. To us that isn't the full availability story, so when you hear us talk about the average recovery times in a DB2 pureScale environment, we include this kind of stuff. Why? Because it matters; and it's because it matters that a lot of engineering went into being able to very quickly find hardware or software failures in the DB2 pureScale cluster while at the same time minimizing false-down scenarios.

The Global Buffer Pool as a Page Cache
During Member Crash Recovery

The CF server's GBP facility provides a distinct advantage compared to competitive solutions with respect to transaction log-based recovery times. In DB2 pureScale, transactional commit processing involves writing all committed data (from the local buffer pools) to the GBP, thereby ensuring that only a bare minimum of transaction log-based recovery is necessary. This minimization is achieved because log records relating to transactions that have committed are simply skipped, and pages read from the GBP during MCR that pertain to such log records indicate to the database engine that the changes have already been applied. In addition, and more importantly, the vast majority of pages that need to be examined (or modified) during log-based REDO and UNDO are obtained by the member performing the MCR process directly from the GBP *without* necessitating I/O from disk. Traditionally, database recovery performance tends to be bottlenecked by the random I/Os that log-based REDO and UNDO requires. Since the GBP serves as a store-in cache for the DB2 pureScale cluster, it pretty much eliminates the vast majority of page I/O that would otherwise have been required for MCR (and is likely required in competing solutions).

Ultra-Fast I/O Fencing

Any kind of cluster services software, including DB2 Cluster Services, determines the health of a host computer that participates in a cluster based on its ability to send and receive heart-beat messages at some predetermined interval. A host computer that doesn't respond to these sent and received messages is eventually considered to have failed; however, even though the host computer isn't responding to these heart-beat messages, it may still have access to the shared disk and its data.

When a DB2 member fails, DB2 pureScale won't begin the process of MCR on the errant host computer until it can be assured that the failed host computer will not write to the shared database storage (to avoid a corruption of data). The technique used to obtain this assurance is known as *I/O fencing*. If you have experience in the clustering and high-availability world, you know that the condition where one or more cluster constituents become unresponsive to the rest of the cluster's citizens (perhaps as a result of a network error), yet can still access the disk, can cause a very undesirable phenomena known as *split-brain*. I/O fencing is used by clustering software to ensure that only host computers on one side of a network partition are allowed to access the shared disk (and can thus perform the recovery of their failed counterparts) to circumvent the potential split-brain scenario.

In environments that leverage storage subsystems that support it, DB2 pureScale can leverage an advanced I/O fencing technique known as *SCSI-3*

Persistent Reserve (SCSI-3 PR). As of the time we wrote this book, the IBM DS3000, DS4000, DS5000, DS8000, and EMC Symmetrix DMX families of storage controllers support the advanced SCSI-3 PR I/O fencing protocols that DB2 Cluster Services will use on AIX. SCSI-3 PR is particularly efficient with the I/O fencing techniques because it's implemented by a special SCSI command known as `preempt and abort` which executes directly in the storage controller's firmware itself. Being a firmware-level protocol, I/O fencing can be achieved within approximately one second—so it's an extremely fast way to ensure that a failed member can't access the disk and cause data corruption. Once the storage controller has processed this command (which is issued by a healthy host computer that's in the cluster), the controller itself *guarantees* that I/Os from the errant host computer will be rejected. DB2 Cluster Services can then proceed with MCR on a healthy host computer in restart light mode to recover the DB2 member that failed.

Now, it's fair to note that the need for I/O fencing only arises in the rare event that an errant host computer has not failed, yet is somehow unresponsive to heart-beats on the network, but still has access to shared storage. However, since this condition can't be differentiated from the more common type of failure where a host computer simply fails (for example, loses power) and can't access the storage or respond to heart-beats, I/O fencing is always performed in DB2 pureScale since data integrity is paramount (and you'll be glad we designed DB2 pureScale this way).

Not all storage configurations support the SCSI-3 PR modes that DB2 Cluster Services requires to use advanced SCSI-3 PR fencing; therefore, DB2 Cluster services can use an alternate (and more traditional) I/O fencing algorithm. This alternate fencing algorithm is automatically selected by DB2 Cluster Services if it detects (at install time) that the appropriate SCSI-3 PR functionality does not exist (so there's nothing for a DBA to do—which is nice). The traditional fencing approach involves a disk-leasing algorithm whereby host computers obtain a disk lease that is valid for some period of time (typically, for a set number of seconds). Once the lease expires, the host computers are required to renew their lease. Lease renewal occurs over the same network that DB2 Cluster Services uses for host computer liveliness tests via heart-beating. Therefore, an unresponsive (or failed) host computer will also fail to renew its disk lease on the shared disks. After a set number of lease-renewal intervals have expired without a successfully negotiated lease, DB2 Cluster Services determines that the errant host computer has failed and should no longer have the authority to perform I/O (as it no longer has a valid disk lease). At this fencing point, MCR can start to recover the failed member.

This is another area of key differentiation between DB2 pureScale and what's typically used in the competitive products we've had experience with. While this alternate fencing algorithm is good enough to ensure data integrity, the time it takes to fence off disk access with this approach is likely measured in tens of seconds; thus, the database system is unable to recognize that the disk leases have expired for some period of time. Now take a moment to reflect on our discussion of how many competitors advertise recovery times—they're likely not to include this in their marketing hoopla.

Why is this alternate fencing algorithm slower than SCSC-3PR? The alternate fencing algorithm is slower than the one used with SCSI-3 PR because it has to have a safe lease expiry interval that needs to account for cases where a host computer might be bogged down and unable to schedule the threads required to negotiate a disk lease. In contrast, the I/O fencing performed by DB2 pureScale with SCSI-3 PR storage controllers can typically be completed within one second.

The concepts discussed so far in this chapter are informational; but we know some of you techies wouldn't be satisfied without at least a peek into the internal operations of DB2 Cluster Services. From a day-to-day operational perspective, DBAs never have to concern themselves with discovering or setting disk lease expiry intervals and so on: These are internal concepts to DB2 Cluster Services. DB2 Cluster Services automatically detects whether or not the appropriate SCSI-3 PR modes are present and picks the best I/O fencing algorithm it can based on the underlying hardware.

We'll make one last comment here in case it needs to be explicitly said. DB2 pureScale *supports all traditional* SAN attached storage, regardless of vendor, make, or model. The *best* member host computer recovery times (such as a hardware failure) will be observed when the underlying storage controller supports the SCSI-3 PR mode that enables DB2 Cluster Services to use the more advanced I/O fencing algorithm.

Cluster Caching Facility Server Crash Recovery

The failure of the primary CF server results in DB2 Cluster Services transferring the primary responsibilities to its secondary CF counterpart. A primary failover is only possible if the secondary is in PEER STATE; that is, if the secondary CF server has all the information (pages and retained locks) it needs to be able to assume the role of the primary CF server.

In a perfectly healthy DB2 pureScale cluster (assuming you're using the recommended redundancy for the CF services), the secondary server is always in PEER STATE with the primary. The only time that the secondary server won't be in PEER STATE with the primary server is if there was a previous CF server failure or if a CF server was previously stopped for maintenance purposes and subsequently restarted. A newly restarted CF server in both of these cases undergoes catch-up processing after being restarted. At the end of the catch-up phase, it re-enters PEER STATE and is then ready from that point to take over the role of the primary CF server should a subsequent failure of this service occur.

If the primary CF fails, DB2 Cluster Services will first determine that the secondary server is in PEER STATE and then subsequently coordinate the reconstruction of information that was lost when the primary server failed. You might recall that earlier in this chapter we noted that non-retained locks and the GBP page registry are not duplexed to the secondary CF server. For this reason, DB2 Cluster Services directs the surviving members in the cluster to send their lock and page information to the secondary CF server. Once this reconstruction is successful, DB2 Cluster Services promotes the secondary server to a primary CF if this service fails and informs all DB2 members in the cluster of this role change.

During the primary failover, CF services are suspended. DB2 members can continue to service applications until such a time that a member needs to communicate with the CF server. For example, even while the CF services are failing over to the secondary server, a member can continue to grant locks locally to transactions, via the local lock manager, which have already been granted by the GLM (in a compatible mode, of course). Read and write access to the local buffer pool can continue for previously cached pages. If the cluster has to service an application request that requires a member to communicate with the primary CF server, such access will experience a small delay until the CF failover operation is complete. From the application's perspective, it seems as if a transaction encountered a longer lock wait than normal. No errors are returned to applications and therefore the failover is largely transparent to applications.

Once the failover of the CF services has completed, DB2 pureScale members continue to access the CF services through the newly appointed primary (which used to be the secondary CF server). The old primary CF, when it is fixed and restarted, automatically undergoes catch-up processing and assumes the role of the secondary CF server when reintroduced into the cluster.

Group Restart

In the rare case that both the primary and secondary CF servers experience a failure, or if the primary server failed while the secondary server was not in PEER STATE, DB2 pureScale would initiate a special kind of recovery referred to as *group crash recovery* (GCR). In this rare case, GCR denies any application access to the database while it restarts the cluster members; GCR is very similar to crash recovery in a non-clustered DB2 databases. Specifically, GCR processing results in a log merge of all the members' log records, followed by REDO and UNDO processing. Once the database is made transactionally consistent, it is open for access again through the members.

Recovery Scenarios

In the remainder of this chapter, we will walk you through detailed examples of some failure scenarios, and their associated recovery actions that are orchestrated by DB2 Cluster Services, which can occur in a DB2 pureScale environment. *All the recovery scenarios* in this chapter begin with the DB2 pureScale cluster in the same initial state shown in Figure 6.2.

As you can see in Figure 6.2, our sample DB2 pureScale cluster has four members and two CF servers. Each member and CF server resides on its own host computer. It's important to note that we could have easily created a scenario where the CF server software and the DB2 pureScale members resided in LPARs such that the physical host computers had one member and one CF server running on it; however, to keep things simple, we decided to not use LPARs in the examples that follow.

The *db2nodes.cfg* file associated with this cluster is shown in the following code:

```
0    host0    0    host0-ib0           MEMBER
1    host1    0    host1-ib0           MEMBER
2    host2    0    host2-ib0           MEMBER
3    host3    0    host3-ib0           MEMBER
4    host4    0    host4-ib0              CF
5    host5    0    host5-ib0              CF
```

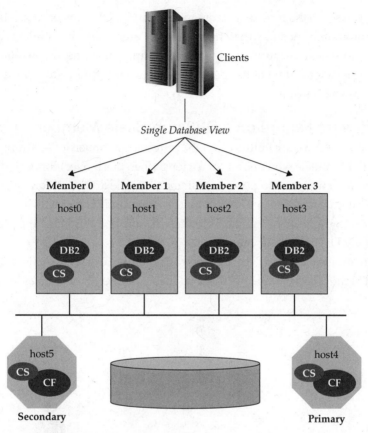

Figure 6.2 *A healthy DB2 pureScale environment*

If a DBA were to run the db2instance -list command in the DB2 pureScale cluster's current state, it would return output similar to the following:

```
ID  TYPE      STATE      HOME_HOST         CURRENT_HOST    ALERT
0   MEMBER    STARTED    host0             host0           NO
1   MEMBER    STARTED    host1             host1           NO
2   MEMBER    STARTED    host2             host2           NO
3   MEMBER    STARTED    host3             host3           NO
4   CF        PRIMARY    host4             host4           NO
5   CF        PEER       host5             host5           NO

HOST_NAME   STATE      INSTANCE_STOPPED    ALERT
host0       ACTIVE     NO                  NO
host1       ACTIVE     NO                  NO
host2       ACTIVE     NO                  NO
host3       ACTIVE     NO                  NO
host4       ACTIVE     NO                  NO
host5       ACTIVE     NO                  NO
```

You can see in the previous command output that the cluster, at this time, is in a normal state, meaning that there currently aren't any availability issues or troubles and the DB2 pureScale instance is running just fine. In the remaining sections, let's look at what happens as troubles are introduced in our sample DB2 pureScale cluster.

A Software Failure on a DB2 pureScale Member

To illustrate a software failure on a DB2 pureScale member, let's assume that a junior DBA (and he won't be junior for long when this is over) connected to the DB2 member assigned to ID=3 (running on host3) and erroneously kills the DB2 pureScale software with a signal 9 command. This causes a SIGKILL of the db2sysc process, which ultimately results in a software failure condition of the DB2 pureScale member ID=3.

You can see in Figure 6.3 that as soon as the failure occurs, work is no longer routed to the failed member by the workload balancer algorithm (as indicated

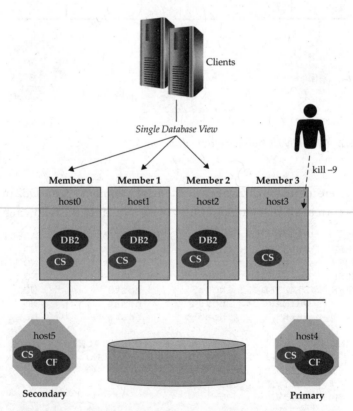

Figure 6.3 *The DB2 pureScale member running on host3 experiences a failure due to a DBA issuing a signal 9 on the DB2 pureScale software.*

by the missing arrow between the clients connecting to the cluster and the host3 host computer).

Figure 6.4 shows the immediate response by DB2 Cluster Services after it detects the software failure that just occurred on host3. We've seen this happen in under a second: We told you there was something special about DB2 pureScale. If you look at some other marketplace offerings, you'll find most measure this detection time between 3 and 10 seconds—and they often don't account for this failure detection time in the recovery time quotations. You can see that DB2 Cluster Services broadcasts (see the arrows connected to the CS ovals) departure notifications to the other cluster members, and CF servers, informing them about Member 3's failure.

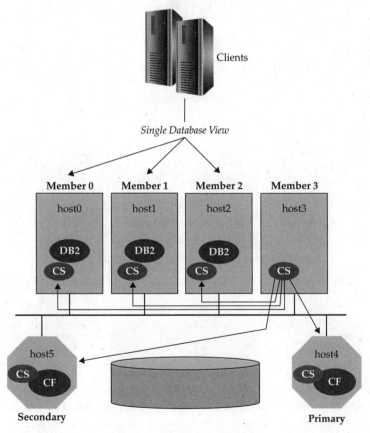

Figure 6.4 *DB2 Cluster Services sends departure notifications to other cluster constituents when host3 experiences a failure.*

This departure notification occurring in the situation shown in Figure 6.4 tells the other cluster constituents to *not* include that now-failed Member 3 in the DB2 pureScale cluster protocols; in response to this departure notification broadcast, the primary CF server (running on host4) also frees up Member 3's non-retained locks.

The next step in the recovery process is shown in Figure 6.5, where you can see that DB2 Cluster Services restarts (we'll assume that in this example, this restart is successful) the DB2 member software on the failed member's home host computer (which the *db2nodes.cfg* file tells you is host3—and of course you can see that in the figure itself). As you may recall from earlier in this

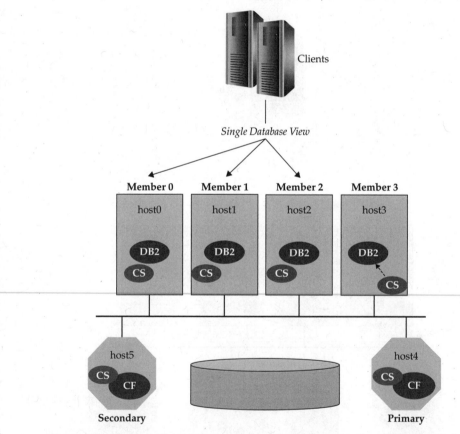

Figure 6.5 *Member 3 is restarted on its home host computer (host3) by DB2 Cluster Services.*

chapter, because the failure experienced on `host3` is software-related, Member 3's home host computer (`host3`) is still considered healthy and the member is therefore restarted where it was running before the failure occurred (its home host computer).

If a DBA were to issue a `db2instance -list` command while the failed DB2 member's processes were being restarted, the output of this command would look similar to:

```
ID   TYPE       STATE         HOME_HOST    CURRENT_HOST    ALERT
0    MEMBER     STARTED       host0        host0           NO
1    MEMBER     STARTED       host1        host1           NO
2    MEMBER     STARTED       host2        host2           NO
3    MEMBER     RESTARTING    host3        host3           NO
4    CF         PRIMARY       host4        host4           NO
5    CF         PEER          host5        host5           NO
. . .
```

Notice that in the output of this command, STATE=RESTARTING (we're only showing the `db2instance -list` command's first section here—and will continue to do so in this chapter if the second section's output doesn't change from the example given at the start of this chapter—see Chapter 5 for full details). It's also worth noting that the ALERT field continues to be set to NO. The ALERT field is only set to YES if DB2 Cluster Services believes that manual intervention may be required to resolve the experienced failure condition. In the case of a software failure followed by a successful automatic restart of the DB2 member software by DB2 Cluster Services, such as the one described in this example, no human intervention is necessary and therefore the ALERT field remains set to NO.

At this point in our scenario, Member 3's processes have been successfully restarted and now the DB2 member itself automatically discovers that member crash recovery (MCR) is necessary since it had previously failed. This initiation of this member-driven MCR is shown in Figure 6.6.

In Figure 6.6, you can see the Member 3 is performing its own MCR, which in this case only requires transaction log REDO and UNDO processing of its own logs. In addition, you can see how Member 3's MCR benefits from the GBP in this figure, too. It's typically the case in this scenario that almost all (if not all) the pages required for MCR processing are cached in the GBP and do not require any I/O fetching from the disk subsystem, thereby making Member 3's log REDO and UNDO processing very fast as very little I/O is actually required.

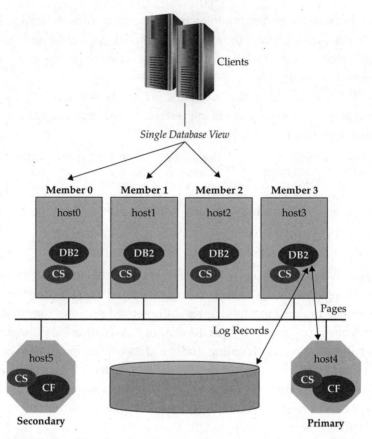

Single Database View

Figure 6.6 *Member 3's performing transaction log recovery after a successful restart*

When the MCR phase is complete, Member 3 is now considered a healthy constituent of the DB2 pureScale cluster—as shown in Figure 6.7. At this point, Member 3 can access the database, and incoming transactions can be routed to it for processing.

You can see in Figure 6.7 that the client connections to host3 have a different line pattern than the other client connections into the DB2 pureScale cluster. As you can imagine, since Member 3 just started servicing cluster transactions again, its utilization is going to be disproportionate compared to the other members. As soon as Member 3 becomes available, application work routes to it, and the DB2 pureScale workload balancer algorithm will observe that Member 3 isn't doing its fair share of work and will disproportionately route new work to it until all the cluster members are equally busy (so the

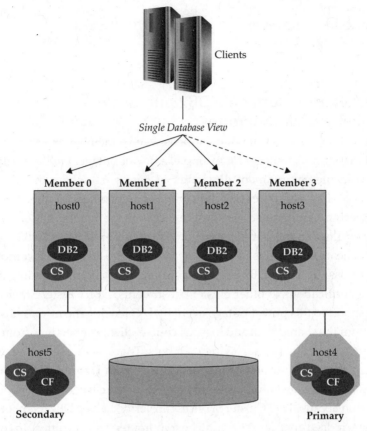

Figure 6.7 *Member's recovery is completed and it can now access the database and start processing transactions again.*

dashed line will become solid in Figure 6.7) in the eyes of the workload balancer algorithm (assuming you're not using affinity-based routing). For more information on the built-in automatic workload balancing in a DB2 pureScale cluster, refer to Chapter 7.

Finally, if you were to run the db2instance -list command at this point, you would find that everything is healthy again in the cluster (see the ID=3 row, which represents the member that failed, has now been completely, and automatically, recovered to a healthy state):

```
ID   TYPE     STATE        HOME_HOST   CUR-RENT_HOST   ALERT

0    MEMBER   STARTED      host0       host0           NO
1    MEMBER   STARTED      host1       host1           NO
```

2	MEMBER	STARTED	host2	host2	NO
3	**MEMBER**	**STARTED**	**host3**	**host3**	**NO**
4	CF	PRIMARY	host4	host4	NO
5	CF	PEER	host5	host5	NO

. . .

A Hardware Failure on a DB2 pureScale Member's Host Computer

In this section, let's look at what happens when a member experiences some sort of catastrophic outage; for example, a power outage. We'll start this scenario with the environment illustrated in Figure 6.8 where the power for Member 3's host computer (running on host3, Member 3's home host computer) becomes unplugged. As was the case with the member-based software failure outlined in the previous section, DB2 Cluster Services will detect the loss of a heart-beat in this case and declare that the host3 host computer is down across the entire DB2 pureScale cluster. In addition to sending out departure notifications to other cluster constituents, DB2 Cluster Services will also respond to this power outage event by I/O fencing the host3 host computer from the shared data and logs. Of course, client connections from Member 3 are rerouted to the surviving members. This is shown in Figure 6.8.

Take a moment now and compare Figure 6.8 with Figure 6.4. In the case of Figure 6.4 (a software failure), it is not possible for the cluster to experience data corruption because DB2 Cluster Services can verify that the DB2 member's processes are indeed gone (as the host3 host computer is still healthy). In contrast, in Figure 6.8 the host3 host computer simply can't be contacted as it is unresponsive. In this simple scenario, Member 3 couldn't actually corrupt any data because the physical host computer has become unplugged from the wall, but as far as DB2 Cluster Services is concerned, the host computer just isn't responding. Suppose for a moment there was a network link failure or an HCA failure on this host computer; to DB2 Cluster Services, such a condition would be indistinguishable from one where Member 3 became isolated from the cluster as a result of one or more network link failures where the member would continue to have access to the shared data. For this reason, we put a question mark on host3 in Figure 6.8. Quite simply, DB2 Cluster Services doesn't really know what happened to the failed host computer in Figure 6.8; it just knows that it can't talk to it, and such a condition necessitates that the I/O for this member be fenced before recovery for the failed member can be initiated.

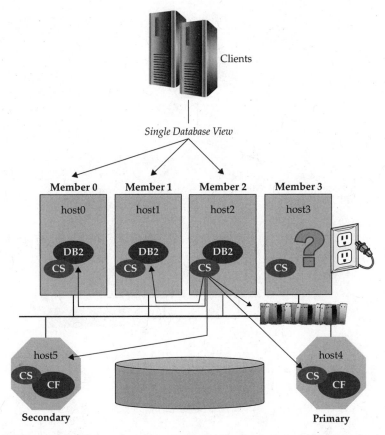

Figure 6.8 *Member 3 experiences a catastrophic power outage on its home host computer.*

The non-retained locks in this example are freed by the primary CF server once it receives departure notification from DB2 Cluster Services. Once departure notifications and I/O fencing have been successfully completed, DB2 Cluster Services restarts the failed Member 3's DB2 processes on another host computer in restart light mode (a concept discussed earlier in this chapter). You can see this in Figure 6.9.

The restart light and transaction log recovery you see on host2 in Figure 6.9 is required because Member 3's home host (host3) is not available to perform its own recovery. To ensure the highest availability of the database, the in-flight transactions that were running on Member 3 at the time of the failure need to be rolled back and non-retained locks held by them need to be freed up to give access to that data as fast as possible.

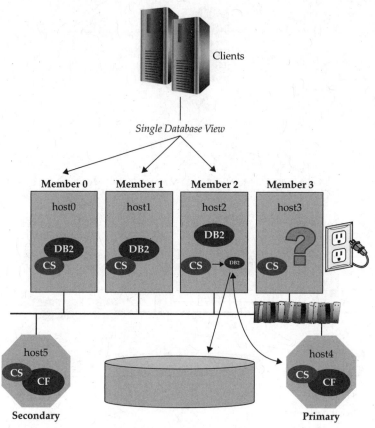

Figure 6.9 *A restart light of Member 3 is performed on Member 2's host computer.*

It is worthwhile at this point look at the output of the db2instance
-list command for this scenario (in this case, we will look at both sections
for reasons that should become apparent in a bit).

ID	TYPE	STATE	HOME_HOST	CURRENT_HOST	ALERT
0	MEMBER	STARTED	host0	host0	NO
1	MEMBER	STARTED	host1	host1	NO
2	MEMBER	STARTED	host2	host2	NO
3	**MEMBER**	**RESTARTING**	**host3**	**host2**	**NO**
4	CF	PRIMARY	host4	host4	NO
5	CF	PEER	host5	host5	NO

HOST_NAME	STATE	INSTANCE_STOPPED	ALERT
host0	ACTIVE	NO	NO
host1	ACTIVE	NO	NO

host2	ACTIVE	NO	NO
host3	**INACTIVE**	**NO**	**YES**
host4	ACTIVE	NO	NO
host5	ACTIVE	NO	NO

In this scenario, you can see that another host computer has to perform the restart light for the failed Member 3, and therefore the CURRENT_HOST field has been changed to host2 (note that there are now two members in the DB2 pureScale cluster running on host2—though one is in running in restart light mode). In the example illustrated in Figure 6.5, since a restart was processed on Member 3's home host computer (host3), this field never changed.

It's also worth commenting on the fact that the output generated from the db2instance -list command associated with this scenario changes the STATE field associated with host3 to INACTIVE because Member 3's home host machine is considered unhealthy (it's not responding to heart-beat messages). You can also see that this host's ALERT field is set to YES (note that it wasn't changed with the software failure scenario associated with Figure 6.5 because DB2 Cluster Services was automatically able to restore the instance without intervention). An unresponsive home host computer (as in the case in Figure 6.9) *may* indicate that human intervention is necessary to restore it and the database instance to a normal operating state.

In our example, while host3 continues to be unresponsive, Member 3 runs in restart light mode on host2 *even after* its transaction log-based recovery is complete. While in restart light mode, Member 3 (now running on the same host computer as Member 2) won't service client connections; it's just running so that it can be involved in future in-doubt transaction resolution processing. In this situation, any clients could issue a LIST INDOUBT TRANSACTIONS command from any member (including Member 3) in the DB2 pureScale cluster and could resolve any in-doubt transactions through those connections.

At this point, as we've discussed, Member 3 is no longer running on its home host computer (host3); rather it's running on what we refer to as a *guest host computer* (in this case, host2 as indicated by the CURRENT_HOST field). If you were to reissue the db2instance -list command at this point, notice the STATE field for Member 3 has been changed to WAITING_FOR_FAILBACK in this command's output:

ID	TYPE	STATE		HOME_HOST	CURRENT_HOST	ALERT
0	MEMBER	STARTED	host0	host0	NO	NO
1	MEMBER	STARTED	host1	host1	NO	NO
2	MEMBER	STARTED	host2	host2	NO	NO

```
3  MEMBER      WAITING_FOR_FAILBACK  host3       host2        NO
4  CF          PRIMARY    host4      host4       NO           NO
5  CF          PEER       host5      host5       NO           NO
...
```

The WAITING_FOR_FAILBACK state indicates that the associated member is waiting for its home host computer to become available again; once it does, this member will be relocated to the host computer where it runs during normal operations and service client connections to the DB2 pureScale cluster. (Note that if you were to examine the second part of the db2instance -list command's output at this point, it would be the same as the previous listing; namely, the STATE field for this member would be INACTIVE and the associated ALERT=YES.)

Let's assume now that the power for host3 is restored and the host computer reboots as shown in Figure 6.10. (Note that its associated member software is still running on Member 2 in restart light mode—the samller DB2 oval.) At this point DB2 Cluster Services will start receiving notifications from the once-failed host3 host computer when the heart-beating associated with host3 is restored. Before DB2 Cluster Services can proceed to the next step, it has to ensure that there aren't any remnants of DB2 member processes running on host3; if there are, they have to be cleaned up before unfencing this member's I/O to disk and allowing it back into the DB2 pureScale cluster.

Obviously, since our running example physically reboots the computer, there is nothing that needs to be done. However, other failure scenarios could involve a situation where the host computer became unresponsive for some time and then became responsive again, as would be the case if the host computer recovered from a networking error but the host computer was not rebooted. In this case, DB2 Cluster Services must perform a process cleanup operation before the I/O fence can be lifted and the once-failed host computer can be re-integrated into the cluster.

It's again interesting to look at the output of the db2instance -list command at this point, which is shown in the following code (we've only included the second section in this output as there are no changes in the first section):

```
...
HOST_NAME   STATE        INSTANCE_STOPPED   ALERT
host0       ACTIVE       NO                 NO
host1       ACTIVE       NO                 NO
host2       ACTIVE       NO                 NO
host3       ACTIVE       NO                 NO
host4       ACTIVE       NO                 NO
host5       ACTIVE       NO                 NO
```

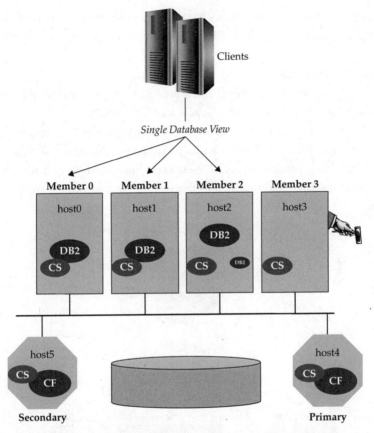

Figure 6.10 *The home host computer for Member 3 has rejoined the cluster, is healthy, and the I/O fence is removed.*

You can see in the second section that the STATE of the host computer host3 is ACTIVE as opposed to INACTIVE, and the ALERT has been cleared and set to NO. This indicates that the home host computer for Member 3 is now ready to get back to its normal duties, as any troubles have been cleared and the host computer is deemed healthy. Member 3 is still not running on its home host computer (or servicing transactions for that matter) and therefore in the first section of this output, it remains unchanged: Member 3 still has STATE=WAITING_FOR_FAILBACK and its CURRENT_HOST=host2 despite HOME_HOST=host3.

DB2 pureScale is just about ready to relocate Member 3 back to its home host computer; at this point, DB2 Cluster Services will quickly perform some additional health checks to ensure that the file systems necessary for operation are appropriately mounted before relocating Member 3 back to its home host3.

Now that host3 has passed all appropriate health checks, Member 3 is ready to go back to its home host computer and be reintegrated into the cluster, and is therefore relocated to it shown in Figure 6.11.

As was the case with the software-related failure, clients connecting to the DB2 pureScale cluster will find Member 3 underloaded (really, at this point, it doesn't have any work running since it's just been started) and work will be assigned to it such that it takes on its fair share of the workload directed at the cluster.

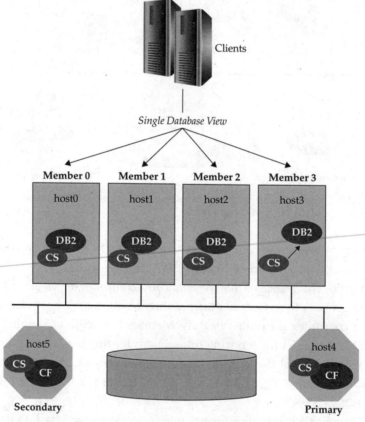

Figure 6.11 *Member 3 is relocated to its home host computer (host3) from the guest host computer (host2).*

As you would expect, an examination of the db2instance -list command output reveals that all is healthy in the DB2 pureScale cluster again:

ID	TYPE	STATE	HOME_HOST	CURRENT_HOST	ALERT
0	MEMBER	STARTED	host0	host0	NO
1	MEMBER	STARTED	host1	host1	NO.
2	MEMBER	STARTED	host2	host2	NO
3	**MEMBER**	**STARTED**	**host3**	**host3**	**NO**
4	CF	PRIMARY	host4	host4	NO
5	CF	PEER	host5	host5	NO

HOST_NAME	STATE	INSTANCE_STOPPED	ALERT
host0	ACTIVE	NO	NO
host1	ACTIVE	NO	NO
host2	ACTIVE	NO	NO
host3	**ACTIVE**	**NO**	**NO**
host4	ACTIVE	NO	NO
host5	ACTIVE	NO	NO

What Happens If a Member Fails to Restart on its Home Host?

As you've seen, a scenario involving an unresponsive host machine is a clear example of a case where restarting a member in restart light mode on another member's home host computer is required; however, there are other scenarios where a restart light is required even while the host computer is responsive to heart-beat messages that are being sent across the DB2 pureScale cluster. Examples of such scenarios (which will all result in restart light processing) include the following:

- **Failure of a network adapter (for example, an HCA) on a host computer**   The host computer may continue to be responsive through heart-beat messages on other adapters, yet unable to communicate over its HCA, which would render data sharing communication with the CF servers impossible.

- **SAN access failure such as a Host Bus Adapter (HBA) failure**   The host computer would be unable to perform I/O to or from the disk subsystem.

- **Failure to restart a failed DB2 member on its home host computer**   A DB2 member fails on its home host computer as a result of a software failure (for example, a signal 9), and DB2 Cluster Services tried and failed to restart it on its home host computer.

In the remainder of this section we'll walk through a scenario where a member fails to restart on its home host computer, to illustrate these kinds of failures.

Let's start this failure scenario with the assumption that the host computer (host3) in Figure 6.12 is suffering from heavy paging activity, perhaps caused by some errant home-grown software with a memory leak.

Some operating systems will respond to this type of condition by first sending a SIGDANGER signal to the running processes, followed by a SIGKILL signal 9 if the situation does not resolve itself. Either way, in this scenario, the DB2 pureScale software processes running on Member 3, which runs on host3, are terminated as a result. As you'd expect, DB2 Cluster Services detects the death of Member 3 and sends out departure notifications to the other cluster constituents.

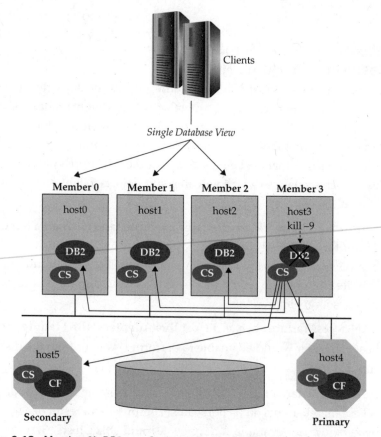

Figure 6.12 *Member 3's DB2 pureScale processes are killed by the operating system as a result of heavy paging activity on host3.*

You can see in Figure 6.13 that the DB2 Cluster Services daemon on `host3` is in the process of issuing the ubiquitous departure notifications that you've become accustomed to when a failed member is discovered and subsequently removed from the cluster. While it's possible that the DB2 Cluster Services daemons could have been affected by the severe paging activity on `host3`, the DB2 Cluster Services processes run with very high priority and tend to only access pre-allocated pre-pinned memory; therefore, it's likely that they can continue to operate normally even under these types of conditions. If the severe paging issues described in this example have impacted the DB2 Cluster Services daemons to such a point that they cannot send out departure notifications, then a DB2 Cluster Services daemon on one of the other host computers will perform this task. Specifically, DB2 Cluster Services detects the software failure of Member 3's processes and immediately attempts to restart the DB2 member

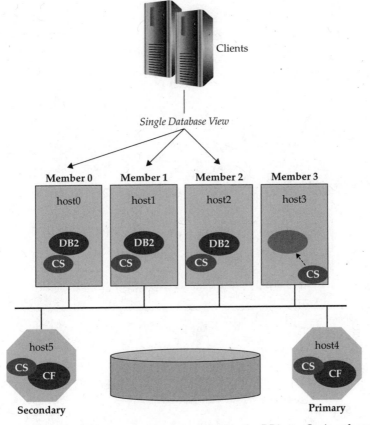

Figure 6.13 *Despite the host computer being healthy, the DB2 pureScale software has failed to restart a failed Member 3.*

on its home host computer. At this point, this scenario is very similar to the scenario described in the section "A Software Failure on a DB2 pureScale Member" earlier in this chapter. However, this is not like the case where the DB2 pureScale software simply failed on the member and MCR successfully restarted it. To make this scenario a little more complex, let's assume in Figure 6.13 that the DB2 pureScale software wasn't able to be restarted (notice that the DB2 oval on host3 that you've become accustomed to isn't there?); we'll assume the restart failed because the host computer was unable to allocate resources (such as memory, processes, or threads) as a result of heavy system paging activity.

DB2 Cluster Services proceeds to restart Member 3 on host2 because it failed to restart it on its home host computer host3 as shown in Figure 6.14. Member 3's transaction log recovery is immediately performed on host2,

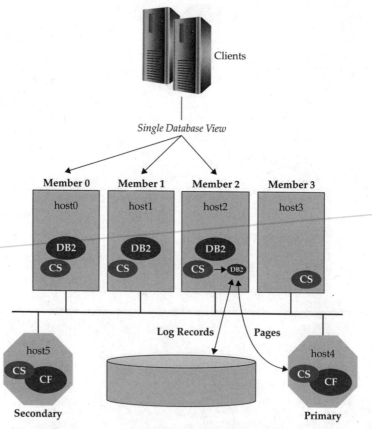

Figure 6.14 *Member 3's restart light is performed on host2 because it was not able to be restarted on its home host computer host3.*

and any retained locks held by in-flight transactions at the time of Member 3's failure are freed at the end of recovery.

If you were to issue the db2instance −list command at this point, its output would show Member 3's STATE=WAITING_FOR_FAILBACK and ALERT=YES. Note that Member 3 will not be automatically relocated back to its home host computer after its transaction log recovery is complete even though its home host computer continues to respond to heart-beat messages in this example. We should note here that DB2 Cluster Services can't determine the reason why Member 3 was unable to be restarted on its home host computer and that's why an alert has be raised; it's intended to notify the DBA that they need to perform some problem determination to understand why the DB2 pureScale software can't be restarted on the home host computer before a relocation can be attempted.

Unlike the member host computer failure case in Figure 6.9, where it was obvious that an ALERT was set on host3 because the host computer's state was INACTIVE, in this case the DBA needs more information. To help get this required information, a DBA can issue the db2cluster −list −alert command—a great starting point. This command will return information similar to the following:

```
1.
Alert: The member 3 failed to start on its home host
"host3". Check the db2diag.log for messages concerning
failures on host "host3" for member 3. See the DB2
Information Center for more details.

Action: This alert must be cleared manually with the
command: db2cluster -cm -clear -alert.

Impact: Member 3 will not be able to service requests
until this alert has been cleared and the member
returns to its home host.
```

Following the guided error-resolution advice, once the DBA inspects the *db2diag.log* file, they will find a db2start failure along with the SQLCODE that resulted from the failure (in our example, it points to a lack of resources on the system). Further investigation into the system logs will indicate that the operating system was running low on paging space at the time that Member 3 was killed. Assuming that the offending application that caused the oversubscription of paging space was rectified, the DBA would then clear the alert using the db2cluster −clear −alert −member 3 command and the DB2 pureScale software would respond with the message: `The alert(s) has been successfully cleared.`

As soon as the alert is cleared, DB2 Cluster Services will attempt to relocate Member 3 back to its home host computer; since the problem with `host3` has been resolved, Member 3's `db2start` command on its home host computer will finish successfully and enable the member to service database transactions on the same host computer as before the failure occurred.

A Hardware Failure on the Cluster Caching Facility Server

So far in this chapter we've talked about the hardware and software failures associated with a DB2 pureScale member. In this section, we are going to turn our attention to scenarios that involve a failure of a CF server.

Figure 6.15 shows the primary CF server's host computer (`host4`) experiencing a catastrophic power failure similar to the one outlined in the previous sections. As expected, DB2 Cluster Services declares the `host4` host computer down since it is not responding to heart-beat messages and subsequently sends departure notifications to DB2 pureScale cluster members.

Naturally, members stop communicating with the primary CF server and failover of this resource starts. During this time, applications that don't require members to communicate with the primary CF server can continue as normal. For example, any locks that were granted by the GLM *before* the CF failure to local lock managers can be further granted to local transactions (in a compatible mode); in addition, cached pages in members' local buffer pools can be read or modified. Applications that require additional CF services will observe a brief pause while failover of these services to the secondary CF takes place.

Unlike the member failure scenarios outlined in the previous sections, a CF server doesn't have to perform any crash recovery, so the concept of a restart light doesn't apply to these servers when they fail. In this scenario, the `db2instance -list` command would show output similar to the following:

ID	TYPE	STATE	HOME_HOST	CURRENT_HOST	ALERT
0	MEMBER	STARTED	host0	host0	NO
1	MEMBER	STARTED	host1	host1	NO
2	MEMBER	STARTED	host2	host2	NO
3	MEMBER	STARTED	host3	host3	NO
4	**CF**	**ERROR**	**host4**	**host4**	**NO**
5	CF	PEER	host5	host5	NO

HOST_NAME	STATE	INSTANCE_STOPPED	ALERT
host0	ACTIVE	NO	NO
host1	ACTIVE	NO	NO
host2	ACTIVE	NO	NO
host3	ACTIVE	NO	NO
host4	**INACTIVE**	**NO**	**YES**
host5	ACTIVE	NO	NO

You can see in the previous output that the failed primary CF server's STATE is now ERROR, because it has become unresponsive. In addition, note that the host computer where the primary DB2 pureScale server was running before any problems occurred has STATE=INACTIVE and ALERT=YES (indicating manual intervention might be required to solve the problem; for example, power needs to be restored to this host computer).

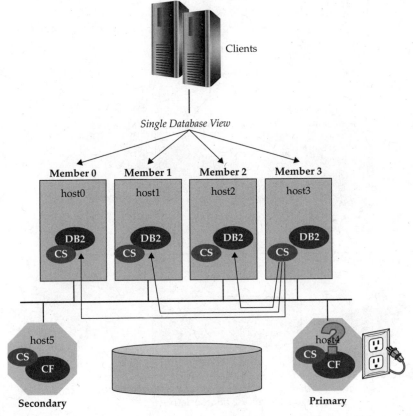

Figure 6.15 *The primary CF experiences a catastrophic power failure on its home computer.*

DB2 Cluster Services now confirms that the secondary CF server is in PEER STATE and that a transfer of the primary's responsibilities to the secondary host computer is possible. Assuming this is the case, in addition to its customary departure notifications, DB2 Cluster Services also asks the cluster's DB2 members to *reconstruct* any missing operational information on the secondary CF server. If you recall from earlier in this chapter, this missing information includes non-retained locks and the page registry metadata. Figure 6.16 shows the DB2 pureScale cluster members sending this information to the secondary CF server.

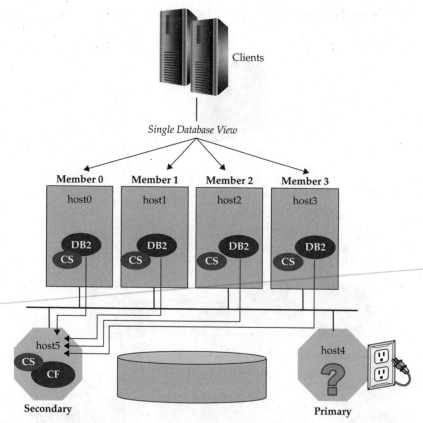

Figure 6.16 *Members are directed to help the secondary CF server construct non-retained lock and page registration information so it can assume a primary role in the DB2 pureScale cluster.*

At this point, you'll note that the STATE field in the first section of the db2instance -list command's output (we aren't showing the second section here because it hasn't changed) for the secondary CF server has changed to BECOMING_PRIMARY while this reconstruction is in progress:

```
ID TYPE     STATE               HOME_HOST    CURRENT_HOST    ALERT
0  MEMBER   STARTED             host0        host0           NO
1  MEMBER   STARTED             host1        host1           NO
2  MEMBER   STARTED             host2        host2           NO
3  MEMBER   STARTED             host3        host3           NO
4  CF       ERROR               host4        host4           NO
5  CF       BECOMING_PRIMARY    host5        host5           NO
```

Figure 6.17 illustrates the situation where the secondary CF server has received all the non-retained lock and page registration information from the cluster's members that it needs to take over primary responsibilities for the

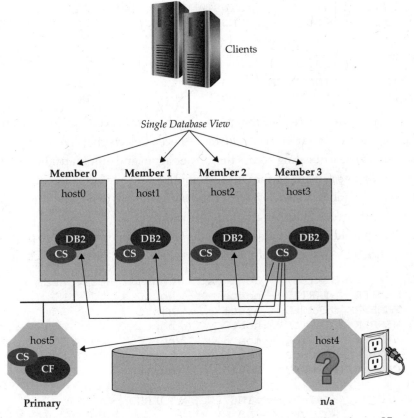

Figure 6.17 *The secondary CF server has now been appointed to the primary CF server and tells the cluster member to continue with any briefly paused transactions.*

DB2 pureScale cluster. At this time, DB2 Cluster Services appoints host5 as the new primary CF server and informs all members in the cluster to continue with any paused primary CF server communications.

You can see in Figure 6.17 that host5 is now the primary CF server; also note that host4 doesn't have any designation assigned to it in the DB2 pureScale cluster. At this point, if you were to issue the db2instance -list command, it would return output similar to the following:

ID	TYPE	STATE	HOME_HOST	CURRENT_HOST	ALERT
0	MEMBER	STARTED	host0	host0	NO
1	MEMBER	STARTED	host1	host1	NO
2	MEMBER	STARTED	host2	host2	NO
3	MEMBER	STARTED	host3	host3	NO
4	**CF**	**ERROR**	**host4**	**host4**	**NO**
5	**CF**	**PRIMARY**	**host5**	**host5**	**NO**

HOST_NAME	STATE	INSTANCE_STOPPED	ALERT
host0	ACTIVE	NO	NO
host1	ACTIVE	NO	NO
host2	ACTIVE	NO	NO
host3	ACTIVE	NO	NO
host4	**INACTIVE**	**NO**	**YES**
host5	**ACTIVE**	**NO**	**NO**

In Figure 6.18 you can see that power has been restored to the original primary CF server (host4). DB2 Cluster Services detects that the host4 host computer is heart-beating across the cluster again and automatically restarts the CF server software on that host computer; it also informs the other DB2 pureScale members that a new CF secondary server has joined the cluster and its metadata needs to be caught up to the primary.

While the old primary CF server on host4 is undergoing catch-up processing, notice how the output of the db2instance -list command changes:

ID	TYPE	STATE	HOME_HOST	CURRENT_HOST	ALERT
0	MEMBER	STARTED	host0	host0	NO
1	MEMBER	STARTED	host1	host1	NO
2	MEMBER	STARTED	host2	host2	NO
3	MEMBER	STARTED	host3	host3	NO
4	**CF**	**CATCHUP**	**host4**	**host4**	**NO**
5	**CF**	**PRIMARY**	**host5**	**host5**	**NO**

HOST_NAME	STATE	INSTANCE_STOPPED	ALERT
host0	ACTIVE	NO	NO
host1	ACTIVE	NO	NO
host2	ACTIVE	NO	NO

host3	ACTIVE	NO	NO
host4	**ACTIVE**	**NO**	**NO**
host5	**ACTIVE**	**NO**	**NO**

Specifically, you can see that the failed (host4) CF server's STATE has changed from ERROR to CATCHUP, the state of its host computer changed from INACTIVE to ACTIVE, and the alert associated with this host computer has been cleared; in addition, the old secondary (host5) CF server has officially taken over primary responsibilities for the cluster since STATE=BECOMING_ PRIMARY changed to STATE=PRIMARY.

It should be noted that if the primary CF server was to fail during the secondary catch-up phase, the DB2 pureScale cluster would have to undergo

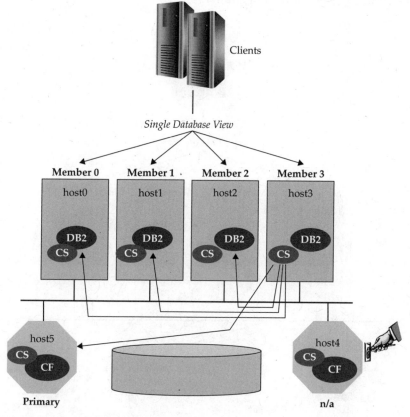

Figure 6.18 *Power is restored to the host computer host4 where the original CF server software was running before that host computer became unplugged.*

group crash recovery (discussed earlier in this chapter). As you can see, even if you were to lose both CF servers, DB2 pureScale has a path to recovery.

Once the DB2 pureScale cluster members are informed of the arrival of the secondary CF server associated with ID=4, they'll start duplexing retained-locks and GBP pages in addition to catch-up processing. The GLM catch-up processing is performed by DB2 members sending retained locks that were granted to them by the primary CF server before the secondary server was reintroduced into the cluster. GBP catch-up processing is performed by the DB2 pureScale members casting (writing) out pages from the primary CF server's GBP to disk; this processing gets the entire system to a point where the oldest page in the primary's GBP has also been duplexed to the secondary's GBP. Once the secondary CF server is caught up, its STATE is changed to PEER as shown in Figure 6.19.

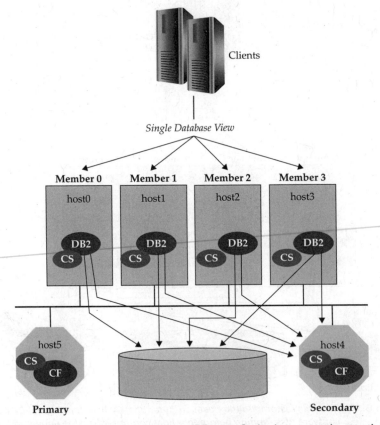

Figure 6.19 *Retained locks are sent by the DB2 pureScale cluster members to the server that is to become the secondary CF server; in addition, pages are casted out from the primary CF server to disk.*

It should be noted that there are other failure scenarios that we've not covered so far in this chapter. For example, what happens if both the primary CF server and a DB2 pureScale member fail at the same time? What if two DB2 pureScale members fail at the same time? We simply don't have the space to delve into the details of every failure scenario, but rest assured, the DB2 pureScale development team has thought about it and covered the possibility when designing DB2 pureScale.

Stealth Maintenance for Planned Outages

With the focus on 24×7 availability to match today's 24×7 marketplaces, traditional maintenance windows are becoming a thing of the past for many key enterprise applications. DB2 pureScale gives DBAs the flexibility to schedule system maintenance *without* the need to negotiate outage windows with business applications through a procedure known as *stealth maintenance*. To support stealth maintenance, a new `quiesce` option has been added to the traditional `db2stop` command for a DB2 pureScale environment. Unlike a traditional database `quiesce` operation you might be familiar with, `db2stop quiesce` allows the DBA to quiesce a specific member, which presumably will be the target for some kind of scheduled system maintenance. Although it's the default setting, we want to note here that you have to ensure that automatic load balancing (see Chapter 7) is enabled. Assuming this is the case, a DBA simply issues a command to stop the target member with the `quiesce` option; for example:

```
db2stop member 3 quiesce
```

Once the member receives the quiesce notification, any new incoming transactions are rerouted to the other active members in the cluster and no new work is allowed to start on it (Member 3 in this case). Transactions that were already running on the target maintenance member are allowed to complete normally. The `db2stop` command only returns a status message once the last transaction has either committed or aborted on the target member. In short, when you declare that you want to remove a member from the DB2 pureScale cluster for maintenance purposes, currently running transactions are not forced off the member: They are allowed to end their lives naturally. You can also specify the maximum number of minutes that a transaction is allowed to gracefully finish using the `quiesce` option; if a running transaction does not finish within this allotted time, it will be rolled back. You can set the timeout to transactions running on a member from one extreme to the other;

for example, the `db2stop` command would wait indefinitely for the transactions to complete gracefully (the default), or you could configure the environment (set the wait to 0) such that running transactions are interrupted immediately.

Once the member has been stopped, its host computer must be temporarily removed from the DB2 pureScale cluster. In other words, DB2 Cluster Services needs to be informed not to use the target member's host computer for any restart light processing should another resource in the cluster fail. For example, if Member 3's home host computer is `host3`, a DBA would issue the following command after stopping the member software for maintenance:

```
db2stop instance on host3
```

We want to note here that the `db2stop instance on <host>` command applies to a host computer rather than a specific member or CF server. The previous command will shut down any idle `db2sysc` processes (which are pre-allocated to DB2 Cluster Services restart light processing); as a planned consequence, the target host computer will no longer be used for restart light recovery. Of course the database is fully accessible to the other members in the DB2 pureScale cluster and at this point, administrators can perform their planned maintenance on `host3`, such as firmware or operating system upgrade, and so on. When this planned maintenance is complete, the DBA would first re-integrate `host3` back in the DB2 pureScale cluster using the following command:

```
db2start instance on host3
```

Once the host computer is back in the cluster, the DBA starts the software on the member using the following command (think of this process as backing out of the action that was performed to maintain the system):

```
db2start member 3
```

Once Member 3 is successfully started, clients connecting to the DB2 pureScale cluster will observe that this member has little or no workload and will direct new connections and transactions to it to balance the cluster's workload. This pattern can then be repeated in a rolling fashion for all the other host computers in the cluster including those running the CF server software.

7

DB2 pureScale Workload Balancing and Automatic Client Reroute

In order to maximize overall throughput, minimize response time, and help support business-critical service level agreements (SLAs) associated with the applications supported by a cluster, you need to balance work across the cluster's constituents (the host computers that make up the cluster). In this chapter, we'll introduce you to the workload-balancing services built into any DB2 pureScale environment.

Basic Workload Distribution in a Clustered Database

One way to distribute work across a clustered database is to leverage simple IP spraying techniques to distribute incoming work across the cluster's compute resources. This form of workload distribution is somewhat naive in that the work spread across the computers may result in inefficiencies and throughput that is significantly less than optimal. For example, consider a clustered database composed of four host computers, and assume that 25 percent of the client transactions are routed to each of the four host computers in the cluster. In a homogeneous workload, where all clients and transactions perform about the same amount of work, this can result in a reasonable balance of work across the cluster; however, in the real world, as we all are all too well aware, not all clients and not all transactions are created equal.

For example, perhaps the Vice President (VP) of Marketing is running a consumer vulnerability reporting job that heavily scans several tables and therefore consumes significantly more of the cluster's compute resources when compared to the resource consumption rate of the more ubiquitous lighter-weight transactions. In such a scenario, the member upon which this taxing report job was routed to in all likelihood would be overloaded with work when compared to other members in the cluster, which are likely underloaded at this point, as shown in Figure 7.1.

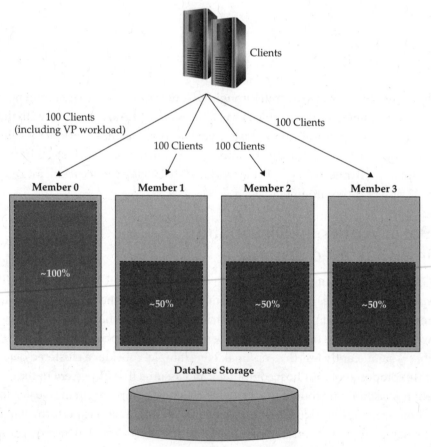

Figure 7.1 *Naive workload routing can result in load imbalances and missed SLAs.*

Note how the client connections in Figure 7.1 are routed in a round-robin fashion across the computers in the cluster. In addition, note that the VP of Marketing's workload was routed (in a round-robin fashion) to Member 0 and is running the very taxing consumer vulnerability report. At the same time, all of the lighter-weight transactions have been routed to the other constituents in the cluster. As you can see in Figure 7.1, even though the number of *connections* to each member in the DB2 pureScale cluster is approximately the same, Member 0 is overloaded because it is running the VP's report.

Consider what would happen now if the IP spraying technique used to distribute incoming workload across the cluster in a round-robin fashion were to route an important lighter-weight transaction to Member 0. Due to the long-running transaction currently running on Member 0, the response times of what should be a quickly running transaction (and the currently long-running VP transaction) are degraded and run a high risk of exceeding the defined SLA for the business. Quite simply, if each lighter-weight transaction is routed to a different member in a round-robin fashion, then the unfortunate ones that land on Member 0 are going to run slower than those that get routed to Member 1, Member 2, or Member 3.

Workload Distribution in a DB2 pureScale Database

To address the inefficiencies outlined in the previous section, DB2 pureScale includes a transparent built-in intelligent workload-balancing mechanism that uses load feedback from the cluster's members to route incoming new work to the members that have relatively low loads currently running on them. This kind of intelligent workload distribution allows the DB2 pureScale cluster to recognize that Member 0 in Figure 7.1 is currently disproportionately overloaded when compared to the other members in the cluster. Therefore, as new work comes into the cluster, transactions are not just routed to another member in round-robin fashion; rather, they are routed based on the load factor of all the members in the cluster. In this manner, the extra load created by the VP's heavily taxing report job will be taken into account when new work arrives at the cluster and is routed across it. As you can see in Figure 7.2, the effect of DB2 pureScale's intelligent workload-balancing techniques result in fewer connections being routed to the member that is running the VP's report. This allows new incoming work to consume the compute resources on the underloaded members and balance the utilization rates across the cluster.

DB2 pureScale's comprehensive set of workload-balancing services allow you to balance incoming workload on connection or transaction boundaries. When workload balancing takes place at a connection level, each database

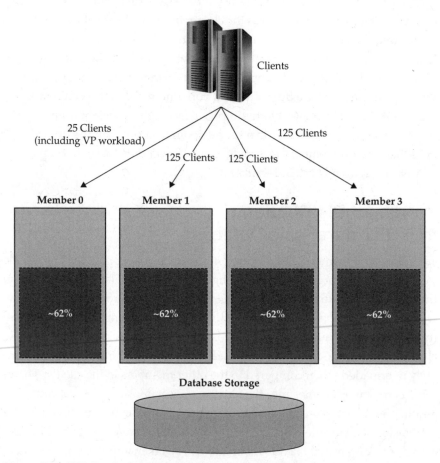

Figure 7.2 *DB2 pureScale workload balancing services provide intelligent workload routing.*

connection is initially routed to a member with a relatively low load, and all transactions execute on that member for the life of that connection. In contrast, with the more granular transaction-level balancing technique, any given transaction within a single connection may be rerouted to a different member, based on that member's load, at a transaction boundary.

The DB2 pureScale workload-balancing infrastructure also reacts to member failures by automatically rerouting connections from failed members to healthy members. (This process is handled by a set of services referred to as *DB2 Cluster Services* and *Automatic Client Reroute [ACR]* and occurs by default, but can be disabled.)

DB2 pureScale workload-balancing services also have an optional affinity-based routing mechanism that you can set up to route work from specific incoming client connections to designated preferred members, instead of automatically by load. For example, perhaps connections from a certain regional application server should always be routed to Member 1, and those from another application server should be routed to Member 2, and so on. With this said, we generally recommend that you use load-based workload routing. Affinity-based routing is best reserved for particular scenarios we'll discuss later in this chapter.

For ODBC/CLI-based connections, DB2 pureScale's connection-level workload-balancing services are available out of the box with default parameter settings that are effective for typical workloads. (As of the time we wrote this book, Java applications could only balance workloads at a transaction level—more on that in a bit.)

In our opinion, if you're pressed for time and decide to stop reading this chapter right now, you're likely to experience very reasonable workload-balancing behavior in your DB2 pureScale cluster with this out-of- the-box configuration. That said, we didn't write the rest of the chapter for nothing, and you might as well invest another 15 minutes to understand the breadth of capability of these services for your DB2 pureScale cluster.

Getting Maximum Benefits from Your Workload-Balancing Services

Even if you're using the default workload-balancing services that you get without any explicit configuration changes, there may be some benefit from additional tuning of the workload-balancing or automatic client reroute services in a DB2 pureScale cluster. Before we dive into deeper details of these options, we feel there are at least three additional options or considerations that most DBAs should know about. To experience full workload-balancing support (and automatic client reroute, for that matter) in your DB2 pureScale environment, clients should connect to members in the DB2 pureScale cluster through TCP/IP since the workload-balancing configuration is based on a target member's host and port.

In some circumstances, workload balancing at a transaction-boundary level can provide a more effective cluster workload distribution mechanism compared to the default connection-level mechanism. For example, consider a three-tier application environment where the application server tier establishes connections to the database up front and rarely releases them from its connection pool (this is pretty typical in a Web-based application). In such an environment, there might be little opportunity for dynamic workload rebalancing at a connection level, making the granularity of transaction-level workload distribution more appropriate for the workload. You can enable transaction-level workload balancing for CLI/ODBC applications by setting the enableWLB element to TRUE in the *db2dsdriver.cfg* client driver configuration file (for Java applications, this element is known as the enableSysplexWLB property). Quite simply, when these parameters are set to TRUE, incoming work is rerouted to different members in the cluster based on overall cluster load on a transaction boundary.

In the *db2dsdriver.cfg* configuration file, there is an element called KeepAliveTimeout (there is no way to specify this in the Java driver; you have to use a system-wide OS level setting for Java clients). Setting this element to a low value (which would represent a low number of seconds) helps the DB2 client detect and react to member failures in a more timely fashion; we'll get into more details about this element, and more, in this chapter's remaining sections.

Finally, the DB2 pureScale workload-balancing services are most effective when each client application is managing multiple connections; the remainder of this chapter gets into these details (including the "Why?" that you may be asking yourself right now).

DB2 pureScale Workload Balancing— More Details and Options

In this section, we delve into more details and options as they relate to the workload-balancing services in a DB2 pureScale cluster. The remainder of this chapter is really aimed at the curious reader who wants to understand the workload-balancing behavior in more detail and the various customization options available.

How Workload-Balancing Information Is Retrieved and Distributed in a DB2 pureScale Cluster

Let's begin with a more detailed description of DB2 pureScale's workload-balancing internals (note that these activities all occur transparently to all applications, just in case we need to explicitly mention this). Workload balancing starts by each member periodically polling each host computer's operating system to get information about the CPU and memory loads on the host computer that is hosting the member (or members if you've virtualized multiple members on a single physical computer). At certain intervals, each member will retrieve the load information from all other members to get a cluster-wide look at the work that's currently running on the DB2 pureScale cluster. This information retrieval is implicitly driven by client activity at the requesting member, and is only done when needed. For example, the load information from other members will not be retrieved at Member 0 if there aren't any clients connected to it; however, in such a scenario, Member 0 would provide its load to other members if asked.

Once a member retrieves the load information from the other members, it will use this combined load information from all the members in the cluster to calculate a relative weighting for each cluster member. Note that the weight for a given member is inversely proportional to its load, and the workload balancer approximates the proportion of the new incoming work that should be routed to this member. Each member then takes the weight it computes for each cluster member and adds the corresponding member's hostname and port number; the combination of all three of these characteristics (the workload weighting for a member, the corresponding hostname, and the corresponding port number) is referred to as the *server list*. At certain intervals, the server list last computed by a member is returned to the clients, which connect to the cluster, and this information is stored in client memory that is allocated and managed by the DB2 client itself; this entire process is transparent to connecting applications.

Finally, the DB2 client will redirect new connections (or optionally, new transactions over existing connections if configured to do so) to members that currently have fewer connections than their weighting calls for. For example, if a DB2 client has a server list in memory with Member 1's weight at 10 and Member 2's weight at 20, it will try to route approximately 33 percent of the work (the weighting is obviously 10/30) of the connections made by the threads using it (or optionally transactions) to Member 1 and 67 percent of the work (the weighting here is 20/30) to Member 2.

Earlier in this chapter, we noted that the workload balancing is most effective when each client application is managing multiple connections; we said this because of the details we just shared with you in the previous paragraph. Specifically, each separate client operating system process (Java Virtual Machine [JVM] in the case of Java clients) manages its own server list. Therefore, all of the connections within a single process (or JVM) are balanced across members based on that process's server list. If there is only one connection from a given client process (or JVM), the DB2 client will be less likely to detect an overloaded member (for example, a member with too many connections assigned to it).

Configuring DB2 pureScale Workload-Balancing Options

As previously mentioned, the various DB2 pureScale workload-balancing options are configured through the client-side *db2dsdriver.cfg* file (or in the case of Java clients, through IBM Data Server Driver for JDBC and SQLJ properties), and in most cases the default settings are just fine for most environments, which allows you to keep the contents of the *db2dsdriver.cfg* file simple. That said, there are several tunable parameters that allow a DBA to adjust the workload-balancing algorithm to the specific requirements for an application.

The following code shows an example of the *db2dsdriver.cfg* file, which enables *transaction-level* workload balancing, with default values for the workload-balancing–related parameters:

```
<databases>
    <database name="SAMPLE" host="myhost" port="myport">
      <WLB>
         <parameter name="enableWLB" value="true"/>
      </WLB>
    </database>
</databases>
```

You can see in the *db2dsdriver.cfg* file that the host and port specified in the <database> element should match what clients specify when they connect to the database (these values may be derived from the DB2 directories). This host and port can map to any of the database members in the DB2 pureScale cluster. If this member is not currently operational when a connect request to it is made, the DB2 client can be configured to make connection attempts to the other members via the alternate_server_list parameter (more on this in a bit).

For environments that require specialized workload balancing, the workload-balancing algorithms can be customized even further. The following *db2dsdriver.cfg* snippet shows a comprehensive example of the available workload-balancing configuration options:

```
<databases>
    <database name="SAMPLE" host="myhost" port="myport">
      <parameter name="connectionLevelLoadBalancing" value="true"/>
      <WLB>
         <parameter name="enableWLB" value="true"/>
         <parameter name="maxRefreshInterval" value="30"/>
         <parameter name="maxTransports" value="-1"/>
         <parameter name="maxTransportIdleTime" value="300"/>
         <parameter name="maxTransportWaitTime" value="-1"/>
      </WLB>
    </database>
</databases>
```

Note the following workload-balancing configuration elements:

• **database name** Indicates the <database name>, server host, and port the configuration information applies to. These attributes should match what clients specify when they connect to the database. The host and port attributes can map to any member in the DB2 pureScale cluster.

- **connectionLevelLoadBalancing**   This setting is used to indicate whether or not workload balancing is enabled for connections to this database. If set to TRUE (the default setting), the DB2 client will attempt to transparently route the connection requests it receives to a member that is below its target connection allocation according to the last server list it received. In addition, when connectionLevelLoadBalancing=TRUE, other workload-balancing options (such as those that relate to transaction- or connection-level boundaries for workload balancing) can be set.

- **enableWLB**   Located within the <WLM> parent element, this element indicates whether or not transaction-level workload balancing is in effect. If enableWLB=TRUE (the default setting is FALSE), in addition to the initial routing of a connection when it's first established, the DB2 client may route the next transaction that is submitted on any given connection to a different member than the one to which it was previously routed (assuming the current server list indicates that a different member is below its target connection allocation, and the connection does not have an in-memory state at its current member that must be maintained across transactions). Some examples of such in-memory states include open cursors (cursors opened with the WITH HOLD option), Global Temporary Tables with the PRESERVE ROWS option, and Created Global Variables.

- **maxRefreshInterval**   Located within the <WLB> parent element, this element indicates how long a given copy of the server list will remain valid for use in a DB2 client. Before a new connection or transaction is routed to a member, the DB2 client will check the age of its current server list. If the current server list is received beyond the amount of time set by this element (30 seconds in the preceding comprehensive sample *db2dsdriver.cfg* file), the DB2 client will request a new server list as it routes the connection or transaction to another member. You might consider setting the value of maxRefreshInterval to a smaller value to have the workload balancer react more quickly to rapidly fluctuating member loads, or to more rapidly exploit new members that come online and add capacity to the DB2 pureScale cluster. You should be aware, however, that there is a small cost associated with retrieving the server list at a high interval rate. We recommend the default 30-second setting for typical usage.

- **maxTransports** This element, located in the parent <WLB> element, indicates the maximum number of *physical transports* (the connection between the client process and a particular member) a given DB2 client can establish within a single application. In contrast, the actual database connections that applications establish can be thought of as *logical connections*. The number of physical transports is typically much larger than the number of logical connections. For example, if a particular client application process has established 100 logical connections to a database on a 5-member DB2 pureScale cluster, there may be up to 500 physical transports established between this process and the members (up to one physical transport per logical connection per member). These physical transports are hidden from the actual client application. They are established and managed by the DB2 client itself (for example, the DB2 Data Server Client or driver software).

  The default value for this parameter is –1, which effectively indicates that there are no limits to the number of physical transports from a client process to database member (think of it as a per-client limit) in a DB2 pureScale cluster; we recommend the default setting for typical DB2 pureScale environments. If you explicitly set this parameter to a finite number, it is possible that a DB2 client may be unable to find an available transport when attempting to route work to a member in the DB2 pureScale cluster. In this case, it will wait for a set amount of time for a physical transport to become available (as defined by the maxTransportWaitTime element—discussed next) before returning an SQL1509N error.

- **maxTransportWaitTime** This element specifies the number of seconds that the DB2 client will wait for a physical transport to become available if it needs to establish a new transport to a member but is unable to find a currently available existing transport and can't create a new transport due to the maxTransports limit or due to a resource shortage. If this wait time is exceeded, without a transport being created or found, a SQL1509N error is returned. The default for this element is –1, which specifies that an unlimited amount of time will be spent waiting for a physical transport to become available if one is needed and no physical transports are available.

- **maxTransportIdleTime**   Specifies the number of seconds (the default is 300) that a physical transport can remain idle before it is removed. Any transport that does not have a logical connection assigned to it within this amount of time will be removed. The pruning of unused physical transports helps to limit the amount of resources consumed to maintain physical transports.

Affinity-Based Workload Routing

Affinity-based routing allows a DBA to designate that work from a certain client gets routed to a designated or preferred member in the DB2 pureScale cluster. Affinity-based routing can be useful for fine tuning or customizing the workload distribution for some DB2 pureScale workload scenarios. For example, consider a scenario with three client machines issuing SQL statements to the DB2 pureScale cluster called *Alpha*, *Beta*, and *Gamma*.

Let's further assume that *Alpha* only issues SQL statements against tables A and B; the *Beta* client only issues SQL against tables C and D, and the *Gamma* client only issues SQL against tables E and F. If all of *Alpha's* connections were running on Member 1, then only Member 1 would need to buffer pages from tables A and B in its local buffer pool. Similarly, if all the *Beta* client's connections were to run on Member 2, then only Member 2 would need to buffer pages from tables C and D. This scenario is a potential workload environment that is naturally partitioned and well-suited to affinity-based routing.

You configure an affinitized workload-balancing scheme in a DB2 pureScale environment using the *db2dsdriver.cfg* file as shown in the following code:

```
<databases>
  <database name="SAMPLE" host="myhost1" port="myport">

    <ACR>
      <parameter name="enableACR" value="true"/>
      <parameter name="enableSeamlessACR" value="true"/>

      <alternate_server_list>
        <server name="m1" hostname="myhost1" port="psport" />
        <server name="m2" hostname="myhost2" port="psport" />
        <server name="m3" hostname="myhost3" port="psport" />
      </alternate_server_list>

      <affinity_list>
        <list name="list1" serverorder="m1,m2,m3" > </list>
        <list name="list2" serverorder="m2,m3,m1" > </list>
```

```
      <list name="list3" serverorder="m3,m1,m2" > </list>
    </affinity_list>

    <client_affinity_defined>
      <client name="alpha"
        hostname="alpha.torolab.ibm.com" listname="list1" >
      </client>
  <client name="beta"
        hostname="beta.torolab.ibm.com" listname="list2" >
      </client>
  <client name="gamma"
        hostname="gamma.torolab.ibm.com" listname="list3" >
      </client>
    </client_affinity_defined>

  </ACR>

</database>
</databases>
```

In this configuration, you can see that *Alpha* is mapped to Member 1 in the DB2 pureScale cluster, *Beta* is mapped to Member 2, and *Gamma* to Member 3. If Member 1 fails, *Alpha's* connections are all automatically rerouted first to Member 2; if Member 2 is also not operational, then they are routed to Member 3. Once Member 1 is operational again, the *Alpha* client's connections (and only its connections) are rerouted back to Member 1.

One important consideration to be aware of with affinity-based routing is the cost associated with analyzing applications to determine the best mapping between clients and members as well as the cost of maintaining this mapping as the DB2 pureScale cluster grows and/or the applications using it evolve. For this reason, we recommend that affinity-based routing be used only by experts who thoroughly understand the applications that will use the DB2 pureScale cluster and are prepared to maintain the affinity-based routing mapping over time. For general deployments, we recommend either connection-level or transaction-level, load-based workload balancing; after all, DB2 pureScale was designed to be very simple to use and not require manual overrides, so take advantage of all the hard work our labs did!

Automatic Client Reroute and DB2 pureScale Workload Balancing

So far in this chapter we've described how connections are automatically load-balanced across operational members in a DB2 pureScale cluster. A discussion on the workload-balancing capabilities in DB2 pureScale would be remiss without discussing what happens, from a workload-balancing perspective, in the presence of a failed member. For example, what happens to the connection on a member in the event that the member fails, perhaps due to a power failure?

In a DB2 pureScale environment, connections aren't just rerouted for the purposes of load balancing; connections can be automatically rerouted when members fail as well. This failover service is known as *Automatic Client Reroute (ACR)*. With ACR, when a member fails, any logical connections that were using physical transports assigned to that member will be *automatically* rerouted to a different transport and a different member. The DB2 client uses its server list in order to perform this reroute automatically, and the application itself *does not need* to re-establish a connection.

ACR is enabled by default-without any additional configuration. With that said, just as with workload balancing, there are additional options with ACR that may be of interest for some DB2 pureScale environments. These options are shown in the following sample ACR configuration file:

```
<databases>
    <database name="SAMPLE" host="myhost1" port="myport">
      <parameter name="KeepAliveTimeout" value="10"/>

      <WLB>
        <parameter name="enableWLB" value="true"/>
      </WLB>

      <ACR>
        <parameter name="enableAcr" value="true"/>
        <parameter name="enableSeamlessAcr" value="true"/>
        <parameter name="maxAcrRetries" value="120"/>
        <parameter name="acrRetryInterval" value="5"/>
    <parameter name="enableAlternateServerListFirstConnect"
value="true"/>
        <alternate_server_list>
          <server name="m2" hostname="myhost2" port="myport" />
          <server name="m3" hostname="myhost3" port="myport" />
      <server name="m4" hostname="myhost4" port="myport" />
        </alternate_server_list>
      </ACR>
    </database>
</databases>
```

Note the following ACR configuration elements:

- **enableAcr**   As its name suggests, this element enables the automatic client reroute behavior (the default is TRUE, which means it's enabled) in a DB2 pureScale cluster.

- **maxAcrRetries** and **acrRetryInterval**   These elements define how many attempts are made to re-establish a connection during ACR processing, and the number of seconds between these attempts. If these parameters are not set, attempts will continue for approximately 10 minutes, with the retry interval gradually increasing as retries continue. We recommend this default behavior for typical deployments.

- **KeepAliveTimeout**   This element doesn't actually change the behavior of DB2's ACR logic; however, it can be very useful in minimizing the time it takes for a DB2 client to detect and react to member failure in a DB2 pureScale cluster. The KeepAliveTimeout element sets the TCP keepalive interval used with the underlying TCP/IP sockets established by a DB2 client when connecting to a database member. The TCP keepalive interval is the number of seconds of idleness on a socket before a keepalive packet is sent to determine whether the other end of the intended connection is still in an operational state. If no response is received, the target connection of the socket is assumed to be nonoperational and the socket is dropped. For example, if a DB2 client was waiting for a response—and it didn't receive one—it would then receive a socket error, which would then trigger ACR failover services (as opposed to waiting indefinitely for the connection).

  If the KeepAliveTimeout element is not set, the sockets established by a DB2 client will use the system default keepalive interval (which is typically two hours). Setting a lower value for this element (for example, 10 seconds) allows the DB2 client to detect member failures more quickly, without the need to reconfigure the system TCP/IP default (which would impact all TCP/IP traffic and not just sockets established by DB2).

- **enableAlternateServerListFirstConnect** and **alternate_server_list**   These elements can be used to tell a DB2 client to try connecting to other members, if the initial member connect attempt fails. Specifically, if enableAlternateServerListFirstConnect=TRUE, then if the member that matches the host and port in database element is not operational when a connect attempt is made to it, the DB2 client will attempt connecting to the members listed in the alternate_server_list element.

- **enableSeamlessAcr**   Enables the use of transparent ACR (the default is TRUE, which means it's on in a DB2 pureScale environment out of the box unless you specify otherwise). As described earlier, ACR transparently re-establishes an application's database connection to another member, if the original member fails. When this element is enabled, that transparency is extended to the SQL statement itself. For example, suppose an application connects to Member 1 and submits a SQL statement and while the SQL statement is executing, Member 1 fails. If seamless ACR is enabled, ACR will not only transparently re-establish the database connection to another member, but it will also transparently resubmit the SQL statement. This can help eliminate the retry logic that you'd have to put into the application if you want to make the failure transparent to the end user. If ACR is configured to run in nontransparent mode, an application may receive an SQL30108N error (a -4498 error would be returned for Java applications) after the connection has been automatically rerouted. This error indicates that the connection has been automatically rerouted, and that the current transaction has been rolled back; however, note that in this case, it has not been resubmitted by the database recovery protocols and it is up to the application to resubmit the transaction.

NOTE   *Transparent ACR may not always be possible. In particular, it is not possible when the member failure occurs after the first SQL statement of a multi-statement transaction completes, or when the failed connection contains an in-memory state that cannot be automatically transferred to another member in the cluster.*

Rely on the wide range of IBM experts, programs, and services that are available to assist you with DB2 pureScale. Surround yourself with our expertise, our programs, and our offerings. Leverage our Information Management Services, Education, and Support offerings to take your DB2 pureScale skills and solutions to the next level.

IBM DB2 Training and Certification

Find greener and more cost effective online learning, traditional classroom, private onsite training, word-class instructors and industry-leading professional certification. New certification exams are now available for DB2 9.7 for Linux, UNIX, and Windows (LUW) and DB2 for z/OS. Look for DB2 pureScale training courses to be available soon.

Visit **ibm.com/software/data/education**

Information Management Bookstore

Now available! Some of the most informative DB2 books on the market, along with valuable links and offers to save you money and enhance your skills on the Information Management Bookstore web site.

Visit **ibm.com/software/data/education/bookstore**

IBM Information Management Software Services for DB2 pureScale

Leverage the IBM Information Management Software Services DB2 pureScale Capability Service for:

- **DB2 pureScale installation and configuration support**   Our pureScale consultants will install onto your existing hardware, a single DB2 pureScale cluster. This will be followed by a demonstration of your DB2 pureScale environment leveraging a sample database.

- **Upgrade from an existing DB2 9.7 instance to DB2 pureScale 9.8**   Our pureScale consultants will work closely with your database administration staff to identify and address all elements in the existing system prior to the upgrade process. All existing databases will then be migrated and you will get a demonstration of your new pureScale environment from our experts.

- **DB2 pureScale HealthCheck**   A DB2 pureScale Health Check includes an in-depth analysis of the DB2 LUW environment followed by a recommendations and findings report of the results of this analysis.

Visit **ibm.com/software/data/services**

Subscription and Support for DB2

Transform your business to be smarter and more innovative with DB2 Software Subscription and Support. Complementing and protecting your software purchase, Software Subscription and Support ensures that you receive the latest product upgrades and 24/7 standard global technical Support.

As an added benefit with no additional cost, you will enjoy a personalized Support experience using the new, award winning IBM Support Portal. The Portal brings together all of our support resources and tools in a single, easy-to-use interface. The new portal helps you become more efficient at keeping your technology—and your business—running smoothly, ultimately saving you time and money.

Visit **ibm.com/software/data/support**

Get Quicker Returns on Your DB2 Investment with the Accelerated Value Program

To get quicker returns on software investments, best-in-class organizations worldwide take a proactive approach in handling their software issues. IBM's Software Accelerated Value Program can help you be proactive by developing and implementing technology management plans customized to support your specific business needs. Find out how you can go from reactive to proactive, changing your focus from issue resolution to issue management with help from the IBM Software Accelerated Value Program experts.

Visit **ibm.com/software/data/support/acceleratedvalue**

Join the DB2 Conversation

Visit the following links to participate in our DB2 communities online:

- Search IBM DB2 Training and Certification on Facebook and become a fan
- Join the community on channeldb2.com
- Read all the most popular DB2 blogs on planetdb2.com